Visual Basic
for Windows

G000152276

PRISMA Computer Courses are structured, practical guides to mastering the most popular computer programs.
PRISMA books are course books, giving step-by-step instructions, which take the user through basic skills to advanced functions in easy to follow, manageable stages.

Now available:

dBase IV
Excel 4.0 for Windows
Lotus 1-2-3
Lotus 1-2-3 for Windows
MS-DOS
Novell Netware
UNIX
Windows
WordPerfect
WordPerfect for Windows

Alexander Parkmann, Martin Schröder

Visual Basic for Windows

PRISMA
COMPUTER
COURSE

Prisma Computer Courses first published in Great Britain 1994 by

Het Spectrum
PO Box 2996
London N5 2TA

Translation: George Hall
Production: LINE UP text productions

© 1994 Rowohlt Taschenbuch Verlag GmbH, Reinbek bei Hamburg

For the English translation
© 1994 Uitgeverij Het Spectrum BV, Utrecht

No part of this book may be reproduced in any form, by print, photoprint,
microfilm or any other means without written permission from the publisher.

ISBN 1 85365 371 3

British Library Cataloguing-in-Publication Data.
A catalogue record for this book is available from the British Library.

All instructions and program listings in this book have been checked with the utmost
care. Nevertheless, it remains possible that errors (human, mechanical or electronic)
may occur. Accordingly, the writers, the translators and the publisher cannot guarantee
the perfect functioning of all the sample programs. The writers, the translators and the
publisher accept no responsibility for any damage, direct or indirect, which may occur
as a result of using the programs dealt with in this book.

Contents

Foreword

This book presents a systematic way of working which enables you to learn how to use Visual Basic to program Windows applications. Visual Basic is regarded as being one of the most important tools in solving any problems which arise under Windows.

The principle of this book is 'learn as you go'. Projects are created step by step, beginning with a problem or a need; Visual Basic translates these projects into a program. It is not our intention to give random examples: a project must deal with a real requirement, and we do not wish to present a loose collection of detailed solutions. We shall direct our attention to solving the problem as a whole. Accordingly, we shall not attempt to illustrate as many instructions and specific features of the programming language as we possibly can. The Visual Basic manual is there for that purpose. We wish to deal with practical applications.

This underlying structure means that this book does not contain exercises in the normal sense of the word. The projects themselves form the exercises. Of course, you do have the freedom to deviate from our proposals and to improve the projects or adapt them more to your own requirements. Now and again, you will also encounter questions (along with the answers) which provide an opportunity to test the knowledge you have acquired.

We wish to thank Carola Henning for her advice concerning the compilation of this book and the manuscript corrections, and Ilse Parkmann for her wonderful practical support.

Alexander Parkmann
Martin Schröder

1 Working with Visual Basic

We presume that you have had some experience of working under Windows and that Visual Basic is already installed on your harddisk C:. If necessary, consult Appendix A about the installation.

Those who have not worked with Visual Basic previously are advised to read Appendix B before beginning. This provides a brief outline of the most important concepts in Visual Basic and a summary of the interface windows in the package.

1.1 First steps with Visual Basic

When Visual Basic has been started up, various windows appear on the Desktop (see the illustration below).

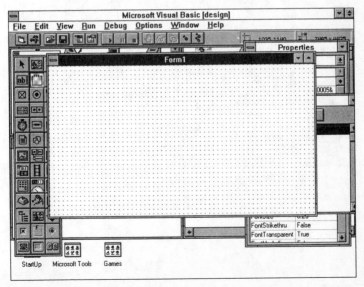

Although the Visual Basic package generates many
windows, keep calm. Everything will fall into place.

You can tidy up the screen a bit by reducing the Program Manager to an icon. You can make this reduction
the default (standard) setting by opening the *Options*
menu of the Program Manager and clicking on the *Min-
imize on Use* option· (Alt-O, M). If you then open the
Options menu once more, you will see that a tick has
been placed in front of that option: this mode will also
be active the next time. This mode ensures that the
Program Manager is automatically reduced to an icon
when an application is started. When Visual Basic is
started up, the Program Manager icon is subsequently
displayed in the lower left-hand corner of the Desktop.

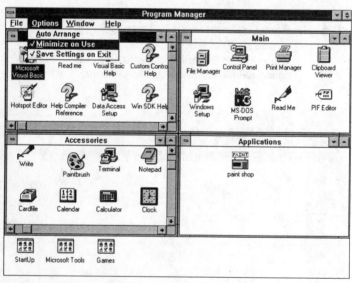

If you are going to work mainly with Visual Basic, you can begin with a clear Desktop by including the program in the StartUp standard program group. Copy Visual Basic to that group by dragging the icon while holding down the Ctrl key. This results in only Visual Basic windows and the Program Manager icon being shown on the Desktop when Windows is started up (plus any other programs which you have included in the StartUp program group).

The Visual Basic program assumes that you wish to come to terms with a new need. The program which is going to resolve this requirement is managed as a project and accordingly, this requirement is assigned the (standard) name Project1. A project consists of various files which are gathered in a project window with the name of the current project.

If the Project window is hidden behind other windows, you can bring it to the foreground using the *Project* command from the *Window* menu (Alt-W, R).

In each project there is at least one window which is referred to as *Form* by Visual Basic. This automatically created form receives the name Form1. The Form1 window has a large number of *properties*: name, position, height, width etc. The parameters of the current form are registered by Visual Basic in a separate window called *Properties*. In theory, Form1 is already a program which provides an empty window with the basic Windows Functions (such as: dragging, minimizing, closing). However, you can do little with such an empty shell. Accordingly, the window should be filled with *controls*, each of which carries out its own particular task. The controls provided by Visual Basic are gathered in the *Toolbox* window which is generally situated at the left-hand side of the screen.

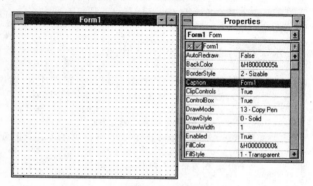

Note: The following illustration shows the extended toolbox in the Professional Edition of Visual Basic. The standard version consists of two columns which contain the controls from Pointer down to OLE 2.0. The controls between brackets are Custom Controls, which are part of the Professional Edition.

Pointer	Picture box	Label
Text box	Frame	Command button
Check box	Option button	Combo box
List box	Horizontal scroll bar	Vertical scroll bar
Timer	Drive list box	Directory list box
File list box	Shape	Line
Image	Data	Grid
OLE 2.0	(Animated button)	Common dialog
(Crystal report)	(Gauge)	(Graph)
(Key status)	(Communications)	(Masked edit)
(Outline)	(Picture clip)	(Spin button)
(3D Check box)	(3D frame)	(3D option button)
(3D command button)	(3D panel)	(3D group push button)

We shall discuss the application of the various tools at the appropriate time when dealing with the example projects.

The Design window in Visual Basic is one level higher in the hierarchy: all other windows are managed from this window.

The Design window consists of a menubar and a tool-bar. You probably know the principle of this combination from working with Windows: the toolbar contains buttons which enable you to give frequently-used commands directly; these commands can also be given via the menus.

 = File Menu, Open Project

Beginning systematically

Visual Basic has the reputation of being easy to apply in order to create a graphic user interface (GUI) for a program. This is true, but that does not mean that a program, when developed, is completely rounded off. Programming is often a matter of constant refinement and improvement.

The *trial and error* method may have the advantage that it will produce results quickly, but if you want to create an orderly and extendable project, an action plan is absolutely necessary.

The first stage in this planned course is to create a separate directory for a new project. If you do not do this, you run the risk of losing data from a previous project. This is because Visual Basic assigns a standard name

to a new project, and new files are written over the old
ones. Therefore you must always specify a new name
for the new file. But if you happen to forget to do so and
then save your file, you will lose your previous file. For
this reason, it is advisable to create a separate directory for each new project. Then the files cannot over-
lap.

For the examples in this book we shall use a basic directory with the name VB_EXMPL. We shall store the
projects in subdirectories with names which indicate
the nature of the projects: ICON_TV, ICONLIST, MC
and ADDRESS. Proceed as follows:

1   Switch to the Program Manager and open the File
     Manager.
2   Select drive C: or another harddisk.
3   Activate the root directory by clicking on it.

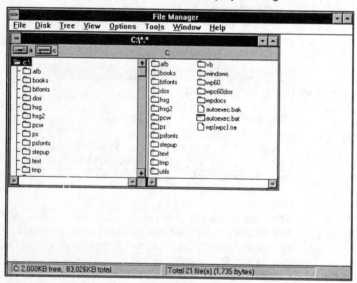

4   Open the *File* menu and give the command *Create
     Directory* (Alt-F, E).

5 Type the name VB_EXMPL in the text box and confirm by clicking on *OK*.

6 Now activate the new directory by double clicking on it and create four new directories for our projects (ICON_TV, ICONLIST, MC and ADDRESS), in the same way as just described.

7 Close the File Manager by clicking on *Exit* in the *File* menu (Alt-F, X or Alt-F4).

The next step is to switch the Visual Basic default directory from C:\VB to C:\VB_EXMPL.

8 In the Program Manager, open the window of the *Visual Basic 3.0* program group (or the *StartUp* program group if Visual Basic is automatically started up by the Program Manager).

9 Mark the Visual Basic icon.

10 Open the *File* menu and click on *Properties* (Alt-F,P or Alt-Enter).

11 Press Tab twice to activate the *Working Directory* field.

12 Specify the new working directory VB_EXMPL.

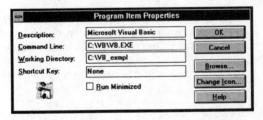

13 Conclude the input by clicking on *OK*.

This alteration only takes effect the next time Visual Basic is started up.

14 Reduce the Program Manager to an icon.

15 Close Visual Basic by clicking on *Exit* in the *File* menu (Alt+F,X).

Note: Alt-F4 only closes the currently active window in
Visual Basic.

16 Start up Visual Basic again.

Notes concerning the examples

We presume that you will want to use Visual Basic for
programming to suit your requirements in the future.
For this reason, we have formulated the examples in
such a way that they produce a finished and working
result.

In the first example, we shall create an *icon viewer*
which enables you to examine icons. The second example proceeds along the same lines and displays a
summary of files with Windows images. The third project contains a file management program for sound devices. In the fourth project we shall construct a simple
address administration system based on the Visual Basic databank module *Data Manager*.

Just to be clear, we shall employ the following rules
when discussing the various types of names, terms
and concepts which are used in Visual Basic:

■ *Commands* and *references* or *keywords* in the normal text are presented in *italics*.
■ Program listings (or parts of these) are
   presented in a non-proportional font.
   Program lines which are new in the listings and which have to be added are presented in **boldface**.
■ The names of Controls will simply be given with a
   capital letter.
■ Names of variables, procedures and properties are
   presented as they are shown in the listings and
   lists, in other words, with one or more capitals.

■ The ⇔ symbol at the beginning of a line of program
   code means that this line is a continuation of the
   previous one: lines like these should be written as
   one line, without pressing Enter.

The project action plan

Prior to beginning with the first project, we shall sum up
the four stages which have to be carried out succes-
sively in order to achieve an executable program.

■ Describe the project in terms of the requirements.
■ Create the graphic work area.
■ Define the properties.
■ Write the program code.

1.2   The ICON_TV project

One of many

We admit that it may not be very original to program an
icon viewer. Nevertheless, because you require this
sort of module in almost every Windows application
and because something like this is very easy to program using Visual Basic, an icon viewer is a very suitable project with which to begin. The result will form the
point of departure for the second project, ICONLIST, in
chapter 2.

1.3   ICON_TV, the project description

When the ICON_TV project has been completed, it will
be able to find icon files on a disk and display a marked
file as an icon on the screen. In addition, the program
should be able to show the file name, the current drive
and directory of this icon. In anticipation of the result,
we shall give an example of this:

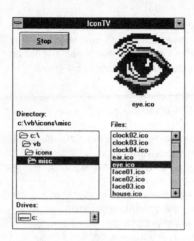

We shall make use of the following controls in this project:

■ **Form**
The *Form1* window is the work area; this is the shell which contains the controls and within which (a module of) the program is created.

■ **Command button**
By means of the Command button control, the program user gives the program the command to start, end or interrupt an action. In the example we shall use a command button to close down the program in an orderly way.

■ **Image**
The Image control enables you to display a file with an image. We shall use this control to display an icon.

■ **Drive list box**
The Drive list box control indicates the currently active drive where the application user is working.

- **Directory list box**
  The Directory list box control generates an options list consisting of a hierarchical scheme of the directories in the currently active drive.

- **File list box**
  The File list box control generates an options list of the files in the currently active directory. In the figure above, only the icon files are shown (with the extension ICO).

- **Label**
  The Label control places a text in a form; this text cannot be altered. This may be a note, a caption or a description. This control enables ICON_TV to supply relevant information, such as the current file name.

1.4   ICON_TV, creating the work area

Activate the empty form window *Form1* by clicking on the dotted work area, or maximize the *Form1* icon by double clicking on it. The title bar is then displayed with a blue background, which indicates that the window is ready to receive controls. There are two methods of placing controls in the form window:

Method 1: Double click
By double clicking on the Command button in the toolbox you can create the required control. This control is automatically placed in the middle of the currently active form.

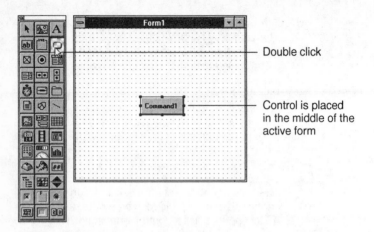

Double click

Control is placed
in the middle of the
active form

Method 2: Marking and opening a control
Mark the button of the required control (a Command
button in our figure) by clicking on it (once). As soon as
the mouse pointer enters the form window, it changes
into a position cross. The cross itself becomes the
starting point for the new control. If you hold down the
mouse button while moving the mouse, the program
draws a frame with a thick grey line. In contrast to the
previous method, you can now directly influence the
size of the control.

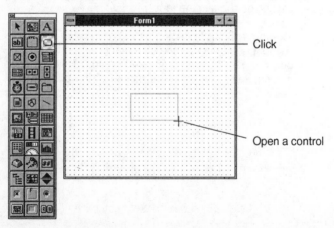

Click

Open a control

Create the first control by means of a double click on the Command button in the toolbox. A button appears in the form, displaying the text Command1. This button is surrounded by a frame with eight small blocks (handles). You can drag a corner or a side of the rectangle by means of these handles: the mouse pointer changes into a two-headed arrow, just as with a window. Drag one of these handles if you wish to give the button a different size.

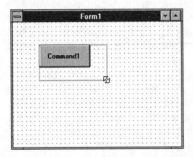

As soon as you release the mouse button, the Command button in the form assumes the size of the frame you have just dragged. Delete this enlarged button by pressing the Del key. Place a new button with the standard size in the form again by double clicking on the Command button in the toolbox once more. Place the mouse pointer on the button and drag it to the top left-hand corner of the form.

Note: The *Undo* command from the *Edit* menu (Alt-E,U or Ctrl-Z) enables you to undo an unintentional action *as long as you have not changed anything else.*

The handles of the control disappear when you click anywhere on the dotted background of the form; it is no longer activated and you cannot make alterations to it. However, if you click on the control, you activate it again. If you hold down the Shift key or the Ctrl key and then mark various controls, you can delete or move

them all in one go, as a group. If more than one control
is activated, the handles are shown in grey.

If the controls are arranged in a convenient way, you
can mark them all using a frame. Place the mouse
pointer on a free area in the work area and drag a
frame so that all the required controls are touched or
enclosed by the frame. As soon as you release the
mouse button, the controls are displayed with grey
handles. However, this method will not be useful in
cases where unwanted controls are located between
those required. Then you will have to use the method
with the Shift key. Try out all these possibilities.

 In order to be able to display the icons we need the Image control. Therefore, double click on the button for
this control in the toolbox. You will recognize this button by the fact that it represents a painting or picture.
Place this control next to the *Command1* button. This
is easily done because the top handles coincide with
the grid points in the form.

Saving

Do not forget to save the results of your work in between times. You have to do this yourself, Visual Basic
does not do this automatically. Never run a provisional
version of a program before having saved it. The harddisk always only contains the version which was last
saved. If you are working away enthusiastically, that
may be a version from quite a while ago!

Save the file by selecting the *Save Project As* option
from the *File* menu (Alt-F,E). Each form is a logical unit
and is saved as a separate file. For this reason, Visual
Basic always asks for the filenames of modified forms
(recognizable by the FRM extension) first. Only then
does Visual Basic ask for the name of the project. The
project file (recognizable by the MAK extension) contains a summary of the files which are part of the project. Proceed as follows:

1   Give the command *Save Project As* from the *File*
    menu (Alt-F,E).

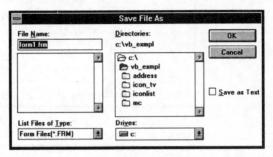

2   Switch to the ICON_TV directory.
3   Replace the default name FORM1.FRM with our
    form name ICON_TV and confirm this by pressing
    Enter.

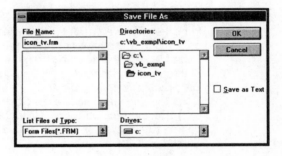

4   A dialog window automatically follows which pro-
    poses the name PROJECT1.MAK as the project
    name. Change this name to ICON_TV.MAK and
    confirm it by pressing Enter or clicking on *OK*.

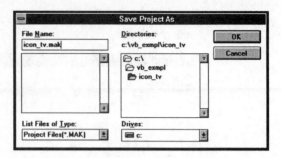

Closing Visual Basic, starting up again and opening an existing project

Now perform the following actions to practise closing down and starting up Visual Basic, and also opening existing projects:

1   Close Visual Basic by selecting the *Exit* command from the *File* menu (Alt-F,X). If alterations have been made which have not yet been saved, Visual Basic will state this in a dialog box.

2   Start up Visual Basic again. The program automatically presents a new project.

3   Open the *File* menu and select *Open Project* (Alt-F,O). Double click on ICON_TV in the directories box and then click on ICON_TV.MAK in the File Name box. Click on *OK*.

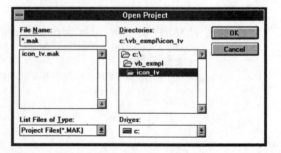

4   Visual Basic generates the project window in
     which the name of the ICON_TV.FRM form is
     marked. If this project window is not shown directly
     on your screen, open the *Window* menu and click
     on *Project*. Behind the file name in the project win-
     dow, the default name Form1 is still shown. This is
     the name which appears at the top of the form win-
     dow. Open this form for further editing by clicking
     on the *View Form* button.

Note: The project window contains (in the Standard
         Edition) the files CMDIALOG.VBX, GRID.VBX
         and MSOLE2.VBX in addition to the form file.
         Visual Basic automatically adds these files to a
         project. In the Professional Edition a greater
         number of VBX files are available; see the tool-
         box in section 1.1. A file with the extension VBX
         executes the procedure which is symbolized by
         a control. To obtain additional information about
         the control files, consult Appendix B.

After this small digression we shall complete the form
by adding more controls. Three components are
needed to manage a file: the drive name, the directory

name and the name of the file itself. Visual Basic has ready-made controls for these.

We shall begin with the diskdrives. Double click on the Drive list box icon.

 All drives in the system can be displayed by means of this control (by clicking on the scroll arrow), but normally only the currently active drive is visible. If necessary, widen the control to show the label name of the drive. Place this control in the lower left-hand corner.

In the design mode, the Drive list box displays only the currently active drive, but if you execute a program, the control shows a list of all available drives.

Always save the most recent changes to a new provisional version of a program first: this prevents this version being lost if the system gets jammed due to a programming fault!

Start the provisional version of the program by giving the *Start* command from the *Run* menu (Alt-R,S or F5).

The toolbox is closed and the dotted grid in the form window disappears. the Image control box is also invisible. Click on the drives list: you see that also an incomplete program can be executed.

If you click on the *Command1* button, the drives list closes; nothing more happens. This is because this element is still an empty interface: there is no program code with this command. The command can only be executed when the interface has been filled in.

Quit the execution mode by giving the *End* command
from the *Run* menu (Alt-R,E). This will return you to the
design mode with the grid form.

Double click on the folder icon in the toolbox to place a
Directory list box in the form. Shift this element to the
left-hand side of the form and enlarge it until there is
enough room for at least four directory registrations.
Since the list actually contains six registrations, the
frame for this list is too small. In such cases, Visual Basic automatically adds a scroll bar to the right-hand
side of the window so that you can browse through the
list (we assume that you have created four directories
for the example projects as described). Start the program and check if this element works.

Make a File list box in the form in the same way. The
new element does not contain any names because the
current directory (C:\VB_EXMPL) does not contain any
files. Make this box just as large as the list of directories and place the new element next to the directories
list.

In principle we now have sufficient elements to meet
our needs but a couple of things are still missing, such
as legends and a separate display of chosen registrations.

The Label control enables you to add legends, short
texts and remarks. Make five of these elements in the
free space in the form. Save the project in its present
state.

We have now completed the first stage of the project.

1.5   ICON_TV, defining properties

Each form and all controls have separate properties
such as colour, size and position on the screen. These
properties are managed for each object in the *Properties* window. This window displays the properties set-

tings of the marked object. If more than one object is marked at one time, the window only shows the shared properties of those objects.

Bring the *Properties* window to the foreground by selecting the *Properties* from the *Window* menu (Alt-W,O). You can also do this by pressing F4 or by clicking on a visible part of the window.

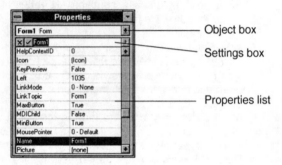

Object box

Settings box

Properties list

The window has three components:

■   The *Object box* shows the currently active form or control. By clicking on the scroll arrow, you open an alphabetical list of the active form and all the controls in this form.

■   In the *Settings box* you alter the values of the activated property of the activated object. The scroll arrow at the right-hand side of the field opens a list containing values which are valid for this property.

If the scroll arrow is (almost) invisible, you will have to type the required value for the property in the text field yourself. With some properties (such as *BackColor*), the scroll arrow is replaced by three dots. In that case, the button opens an additional options window. The two buttons at the left of the text field enable you to directly confirm the alteration (tick) or to cancel it (cross).

■ The *Properties list* consists of a table with two columns (generally with a scroll bar), which contains all the properties of the form or the object, which can be altered. The left column shows the name of the properties, the right column shows the current values. The properties in the list are alphabetically arranged.

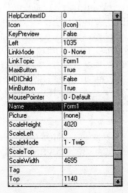

Firstly, we shall adjust the properties of the Form1 form to the requirements of the example project. Open the Properties window and activate, if necessary, the Form1 object from the list in the Object box. By clicking on the lower scroll arrow, you can see how many properties this object has. We wish to alter a few of these.

The position of an object is determined by the properties *Left* and *Top*, the co-ordinates of the upper left-hand corner of the object. This position is always measured in relation to the absolute top left corner of the screen (0,0) which can be displayed. *Height* and *Width* refer to sizes of the form.

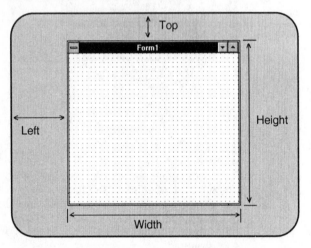

The distances are measured in *twips*. The twip is a unit which is specific to Visual Basic. This measurement depends on the screen being used. Using twips guarantees that the forms and controls in your application always have exactly the same mutual position, regardless of the screen resolution. This is also the case for reproduction on paper. An inch is equal to 1440 twip, a centimetre is roughly 567 twip.

Give the form the following settings:

Left   = 1725 twip
Top   = 1050 twip
Height   = 5730 twip
Width   = 4860 twip

To do this, proceed as follows:

1   Double click on the *Left* property. The default set-
    ting is now shown in the Settings box.
2   Type the value 1725 and confirm this by pressing
    Enter.
3   Repeat these steps for *Top* (1050), *Height* (5730)
    and *Width* (4860).
4   Activate the form window and examine the result
    of the alterations.

The form window is situated a little differently and the
size and shape have also changed. Depending on the
sizes of the labels you positioned, they may or may not
all be visible. These labels have not been lost; they will
become clearly visible when we adjust the values for
their positions.

In the next step we shall adjust the settings for the appearance of the border around the program window.
The *BorderStyle* property of a window can have one of
four possible values:

0   None   No border
1   Fixed Single   Size not adjustable, thin line
2   Sizable   Size adjustable, double filled line
                    (default value)
3   Fixed Double   Size not adjustable, thick coloured
                    line

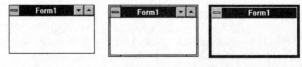

Type 1   Type 2   Type 3

Change the present standard setting to *1 - Fixed Single*. Proceed as follows:

1   Mark the *BorderStyle* property.
2   Activate the settings box by clicking on the arrow to the right of the settings box. A drop-down menu opens.

3   Click on 1. The program adopts the appropriate settings.

Instead of changing the settings in this way, you can also double click on the property. Each time you do this, one of the possible values is entered. Confirm the required value by pressing Enter.

The border you have just specified only becomes visible in the run mode.

When the form is the active object, the *Caption* property defines the text in the title bar of the form window. The *Caption* property contains a text which is only displayed at that place. Enter the name *IconTV* for the form window.

In order to prevent objects being confused within a project, they must have a unique name. The *internal name* of an object is assigned by means of the *Name* property. Enter *IconTV* here as well.

You are already familiar with the fact that Windows applications generally have a Maximize button at the extreme right-hand side of the title bar. This button makes the application screen-filling. An analogous button reduces the window to an icon. The *MaxButton* and *MinButton* properties determine whether or not these properties are available. Both properties can have two logical values: *True* and *False*. The default setting is *True* in both cases. In our example, we shall block the possibility of maximizing the window. Mark the property *MaxButton* and change the property by typing *F* for False.

Save the project before testing the program.

Positioning the controls

The controls, just like the form, are positioned using the *Top* and *Left* properties. In contrast to the form, which is positioned in relation to the screen, the *Top* and *Left* properties relate to the upper left-hand corner of the work area of the relevant form when controls are being positioned. The current positional data are an automatic consequence of where we placed these elements previously. Visual Basic automatically assigns a (consecutive) number to all controls, according to the order of sequence in which they were created. The *TabIndex* numeration begins at 0. The *TabIndex* determines the order in which controls are activated when the Tab key is pressed. In an active form, this order is indicated by the active handles when you press the Tab key. This automatic order can be subsequently altered by allocating another value to the *TabIndex* of the controls. The proper order is usually related to the logical runthrough of the program.

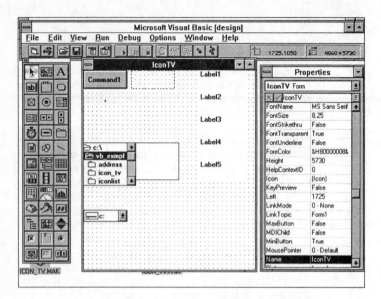

In the *Properties* window, we shall give the controls a
new index (this is also a property). Open the options list
in the Object box and activate the objects named below
one by one in order to adjust their properties as shown.
Press Enter each time to confirm the setting.

Dir1 DirListBox
Height	= 1830
Left	= 90
TabIndex	= 0
Top	= 2700
Width	= 2295

Drive1 DriveListBox
Height	= 315
Left	= 90
TabIndex	= 1
Top	= 4860
Width	= 2295

File1 FileListBox
Height   = 1785
Left   = 2700
TabIndex   = 2
Top   = 2700
Width   = 1935

The Command button with the text Command1 displays a default text which serves as a name. This name is determined by the *Caption* property. Change this text to: *&Stop*. The ampersand sign (&) in front of the S enables you to activate the button by means of the key combination Alt-S. This shortcut key combination is now indicated by the underlining under the S. All objects which have the *Caption* property can be activated in this way.

Change the Command button properties as follows:

Command1 CommandButton
Caption   = &Stop
Height   = 465
Left   = 180
Name   = ProgEnd
TabIndex   = 3
Top   = 90
Width   = 1365

The Image1 window is going to show the selected icon file. Setting the *Stretch* property to *True* converts the loaded file to the size of the control. Setting it to *False* adjusts the size of the control to the size of the image. In our example we shall enlarge the icon in order to be able to see the details better.

Image1 Image
Height   = 1635
Left   = 2790
Name   = Imidge
Stretch   = True
Top   = 120
Width   = 1635

Note: We have given this Image control the name
        Imidge because the word 'image' is a reserved
        word in Visual Basic programming language;
        use of it will otherwise lead to confusion and
        malfunction. The same also applies to the word
        'path' which we shall meet shortly under Label2.
        In that case, we shall employ the name *Way*.

In the Label1 label window we shall display the file
name which is to be placed under the Image field. For
a sophisticated effect, we shall place the name exactly
in the middle under the icon displayed. The *Alignment*
property determines where the text is to be positioned:
0 - Left Justify, 1 - Right Justify, 2 - Center.

When the program is running, we wish the label text to
be shown only when an icon is being displayed; otherwise the box should remain empty. Accordingly, we
shall remove the value of the *Caption* property.

Label1 Label
Alignment   = 2 - Center
Caption   = (empty - therefore press Del)
Height   = 285
Left   = 2790
Name   = File
Top   = 1890
Width   = 1635

When the program is running, the active drive and directory are to be shown in the Label2 field. Accordingly, delete the *Caption* property and change the following properties:

Label2 Label
Caption   = (empty - therefore press Del)
Height   = 285
Left   = 90
Name   = Way
Top   = 2430
Width   = 2535

Note: We have employed the name 'Way' instead of the more obvious 'path'. This is because 'path' is a reserved word in Visual Basic programming language (see the note on the previous page). In addition, the *Name* property must not contain any spaces; accordingly, a name such as 'Current drive' is not correct.

The last three label boxes complete the appearance of IconTV with explanatory text.

Label3 Label
Caption	= Directory:
Height	= 225
Left	= 90
Top	= 2160
Width	= 1215

Label4 Label
Caption	= Files:
Height	= 225
Left	= 2700
Top	= 2430
Width	= 1185

Label5 Label
Caption	= Drives:
Height	= 225
Left	= 90
Top	= 4590
Width	= 1095

When you have specified the values as shown above, the form window will look like this:

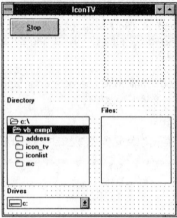

Save the project in its current state and check whether it runs or not.

Check how the individual controls function. It seems that you can switch to a different directory or drive but the corresponding file lists are not displayed. The program will also accept a drive containing no disk without producing an error message. This is the point at which we must begin programming (writing the program code) in order to link the controls, which are still mutually independent, to one another.

1.6   ICON_TV, writing the program code

In this stage of the IconTV project we shall link the controls (with the allocated properties) to one another to produce an executable program. This takes place using commands which have to be formulated according to fixed rules. If you have worked with the BASIC programming language previously, you will have a good point of departure for working with Visual Basic since the coding in Visual Basic deviates little from the instructions in QBasic and QuickBASIC.

The end of the program first

Open the code window by double clicking on a free area in the form window.

Object box   Procedures list

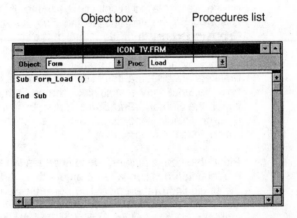

With each object there are specific standard events which are already defined during the creation of an object. When testing the provisional version of the program you will have noticed that, for instance, the operation of the command button by means of the mouse is directly possible, and that this causes movement of the button, but there is no further effect. The program section which is activated by this event still has to be written in the form of a program block: one of the possible *event procedures* from the *Procedures list* is assigned to an event with the relevant object.

The *Object box* contains an alphabetical list of the name of the form and all the controls which have been placed in the form (the allocated names or the default names if no names have been assigned). Mark the *ProgEnd* control in this list. Then open the *Procedures list*. This list contains all the events which can occur in combination with a command button during the execution of the program. In our example we need the *Click* procedure which is marked as the default setting.

Visual Basic assigns a separate program subroutine (program section) to each procedure. A routine begins with the *Sub* command and ends with *End Sub*. The keywords and other elements of the Visual Basic language are displayed in colour. The name of the routine is shown on the first line behind *Sub*, followed by (). The name consists of the name of the object and the event which has been allocated to it, divided from one another by an underlining stripe: ProgEnd_Click. The brackets are added automatically, but in this case they have no function. We shall place the program code between the *Sub* and *End Sub* command lines. Here the program block consists of only the *End* command which ends the program.

Place the mouse pointer, which changes to the form of the insertion position when it enters this work area, at the beginning of the empty line between *Sub* and *End Sub*. Click on the left mouse button. A flashing cursor appears at that position, indicating that the program is now in the Edit mode. Type the command *End* and move the cursor to the next line. When you move on to a new line, Visual Basic checks if the syntax of the line which has just been completed is correct:

■   If the syntax of the input is correct, Visual Basic changes the colour of the input. The syntactic text which was typed in black then acquires the specified Visual Basic background colour (the default setting is blue).
■   If the input remains black when you move to the next line, you have made a mistake somewhere. Check what you have just typed. Occasionally Visual Basic is able to make a suggestion as to what has gone wrong. In that case, an error message appears which will be further explained if you press F1 to activate a help text.

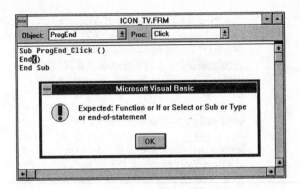

During the development of a program it can be useful to register documentation in the form of explanation. This makes it easier to understand the program code; it often becomes more clear why the code is written in this way instead of otherwise. We shall practise what we preach and add the following text behind the *End* command:

```
'Ends the program
```

The apostrophe indicates to Visual Basic that commentary text follows. As soon as you leave the line containing the commentary text, Visual Basic displays this commentary in green letters.

The ProgEnd routine, when completed, looks like this:

```
Sub ProgEnd_Click ()
    End              'Ends the program
End Sub
```

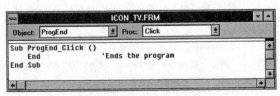

As already mentioned, we recommend including commentary in the program. You can also indent lines within a routine by pressing the Tab key; this helps give more insight into the structure of a program. When displaying examples in this book however, we shall not show commentary in order to avoid confusion with the actual program code. All the necessary explanation will be given in the accompanying text.

Save the project and test the current version of the program. When you click on *Stop* in the Run mode of the form window, the program returns immediately to the Edit mode of this window.

Note: You may have seen that more than one procedure shell is provided in many of the options in the *Procedures list*. You only need to select the particular shell you wish to use and then extend it as required to create the complete routine.

Access to the icon files

In order to display an icon on the screen it is necessary to find and open the corresponding file. The location where the file is stored is defined by the drive, the directory and the filename. In our example we manage these three components of the storage location by means of the Drive1, Dir1 and File1 controls. We shall now begin with Drive1.

The values of all properties which are determined during the design stage are displayed in the properties window. But there are also properties which change during the execution of the program and thus receive their values as a result of the program code. These are **not shown** in the properties window. They are *variables* and thus do not have a fixed value. When specifying the location of a particular file, we must apply the variables *Drive* and *Path*. (See section 1.9 for more information about properties.)

The name of the currently active drive is available in the Drive1 control in the *Drive* property. This property has to be conveyed to the *Path* property of Dir1 in order to inform Dir1 of which drive has been activated. This results in the Dir1.Path element containing information about the currently active drive, and the path to the file can be chosen on this basis.

If you wish to address a *control property* in a program code, indicate that property by naming the control in question followed by a *point* and then specify the name of the property.

Open the Drive1 code window (double click anywhere on the form and select Drive1 from the subsequent Object box of the code window) and place the cursor on the blank line. The program automatically selects the Change procedure which implements a switch to another drive. Add the line shown in boldface to the routine:

```
Sub Drive1_Change ()
    Dir1.Path = Drive1.Drive
End Sub
```

In order to modify the file list when a switch of drive or directory takes place, information about the current drive and directory are needed here too. In the File1 control, that occurs via the variable property *Path*.

Open the Object box in this code window and activate Dir1. Change is the default procedure here also. Complete the routine as shown below and conclude the input by pressing Enter. Visual Basic automatically places the cursor at the indented position corresponding to the previous line.

```
Sub Dir1_Change ()
    File1.Path = Dir1.Path

End Sub
```

The program must display the current drive and the
current directory on the screen in the label window
called Way. To bring this about, we must assign the
contents of the *Dir1.Path* variable property to the *Caption* property of the label called Way.

```
Sub Dir1_Change ()
    File1.Path = Dir1.Path
    Way.Caption = Dir1.Path
End Sub
```

If you now test the program you will see that the Way
label (Way.Caption) remains empty although we did
specify a registration in the Dir_Change routine. Nevertheless there is nothing wrong, because no switch of
drive or directory has yet occurred: the Change procedure has not yet been implemented. This only takes
place when there is a switch to a different directory.

Therefore we must ensure that the value of the currently active path is assigned to the label field when the
program is started up. This is done in the Load procedure which is executed when a form is loaded. Click on
Form in the Object box of the code window. Add the
line shown in boldface.

```
Sub Form_Load ()
    Way.Caption = Dir1.Path
End Sub
```

You may have noticed that we have used this command line previously. In order to avoid unnecessary
typework and the chance of making mistakes, we shall
copy this command to the Form_Load event procedure. This is done as follows:

Open the code window for the Dir1 object. Mark the
command line by dragging the cursor across it while
holding down the left mouse button. The line is now
displayed in inverse video (blue background is the default setting). Now open the *Edit* menu and select *Copy*
(Alt-E, C or Ctrl-C). The information is copied to the

Clipboard. Now open the code window for the Form object and deposit the contents of the Clipboard on the blank line by selecting *Paste* from the *Edit* menu (Alt-E, P or Ctrl-V). Save the program and test it out.

The list of files is to show all the files in the current directory. As yet there are no files in the VB_EXMPL directory, but if you run your program and double click on C:\ a list of files on the harddisk will now be displayed. Switch back to your working directory. For our example, we only require files with the extension ICO for the icons. This also makes it possible to see whether or not a directory contains icon files. If it does not contain icon files, no files are shown at all. We only need to make this selection once, in the Form_Load routine when the program is started up.

The *Pattern* variable property enables you to determine which file names or parts of these are to be selected and subsequently shown in the list of files.

Extend the Form_Load procedure as follows:

```
Sub Form_Load ()
    Way.Caption = Dir1.Path
    File1.Pattern = "*.ico"
End Sub
```

Run the program and switch to the directory C:\VB\ ICONS\ARROWS by double clicking on the appropriate (sub)directory each time. The names of the ICO files in this icon directory are shown in the files list.

We have now reached the stage at which it is possible to display and select file names. However, the contents of the selected file are not yet displayed along with the Image control.

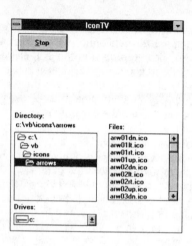

Displaying the icon

In our example project ICON_TV, the contents of the selected file are to be shown as an icon in the Image control. In addition, the name of the file is to be displayed under the icon.

The contents of a label field are managed via the *Caption* property. The marked filename in the Files1 files list is stored under the variable property *FileName*. We shall assign the *File1.FileName* property to File.Caption in order to display the relevant name in the label box called File.

Open the code window of the File1 object. Visual Basic automatically generates the File1_Click routine. Complete the routine as follows:

```
Sub File1_Click ()
    File.Caption = File1.FileName
End Sub
```

The procedure dealing with the display of the icon is analogous to this, but we must ensure that the entire path is added to the chosen filename. The access route to a file, as mentioned, consists of the drive name, the directory name and the actual filename. A part of this information is already stored in the *Path* variable property of the File1 control. We have already recorded the required information in the Drive1_Change procedure by means of the program line:

```
Dir1.Path = Drive1.Drive
```

Other necessary information has been recorded in the Dir1_Change procedure by means of the program line:

```
File1.Path = Dir1.Path
```

The information is stored in the *File1.Path* and the *File1.FileName* variable properties. You could envisage the management system as being a cabinet with drawers. In this case, the cabinet is called File1 and two of the drawers are called Path and FileName. If we open the FileName drawer, we find the filename. If you use the program to switch to another file, the contents of the drawers change. Because the contents of the drawer can change, this element of a program is referred to as a *variable*. In the variable property *File1.FileName*, the filename is managed as a variable of the *string* data type.

A series of random characters in Visual Basic is referred to as a string. Inverted commas are placed at the beginning and end to indicate the starting and ending points of the string. If two sets of inverted commas are placed adjacently, this means that there is an empty string, without characters. A string can have a maximum length of 65,535 characters. A character occupies exactly one byte of memory; the inverted commas do not count. When a string is reproduced on the screen, the inverted commas are not shown. In program code, a string must always be placed between inverted commas.

We shall link the missing filename from File1.FileName to the information in File1.Path. In addition, we must *add the backslash as a separation character* between the pathname and the filename. It is possible to link strings to one another using the & operator.

Note: You can obtain information about the Visual Basic operators in the help screen. Click on the *Search For Help On* option and look under *operators: concatenation* or *& Operator*.

If you want to address the first file (ARW01DN.ICO) in the \VB\ICONS\ARROWS directory of drive C:, the complete access information is as follows:

```
C:\VB\ICONS\ARROWS\ARW01DN.ICO
```

This structure is compiled, in combination with the & operator, using three components in accordance with the formula:

```
File1.Path & "\" & File1.FileName
```

In our example, this becomes the following when converted to text (combination of strings):

```
"C:\VB\ICONS\ARROWS" & "\" & "ARW01DN.ICO"
```

Above, we described the way the pathname which is necessary to find a file is constructed. The marked file is loaded from disk by the LoadPicture() function and passed on to the Image display box. The argument of the LoadPicture function consists of information about access to the file.

The complete routine File1_Click now looks like this:

```
Sub File1_Click ()
    File.Caption = File1.FileName
    Imidge.Picture = LoadPicture(File1.Path & "\"
↻        & File1.FileName)
End Sub
```

All components of the program are fully linked to one another. Save the program and retrieve the first icon.

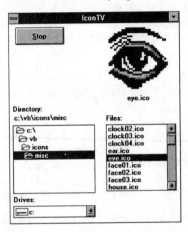

If you now switch back to the ICONS directory, you will see that the chosen icon is still displayed in the image box although the file list does not show any icon files. If you write programs in an orderly way, you shouldn't find that one part of the output does not quite correspond to another part of the output. Therefore, in our example, we wish the icon display to disappear as soon as there is a change of directory or drive. This switch should start a routine which deletes the previous icon. This means that the relevant command will be a part of the Dir1_Change routine. The filename can be deleted by applying an empty string (two adjacent sets of inverted commas) to the *File.Caption* property. In the same way, the image window can be cleared by assigning the value of the LoadPicture function without any arguments to the *Imidge.Picture* property.

Add the new lines to the Dir1_Change routine and test the program.

```
Sub Dir1_Change ()
    File1.Path = Dir1.Path
    Way.Caption = Dir1.Path
    File.Caption = ""
    Imidge.Picture = LoadPicture()
End Sub
```

1.7   ICON_TV, the project files

All IconTV project files are stored in the ICON_TV directory. Each form is stored in a separate file with the
extension FRM. The project file with the MAK extension contains references to the forms and to the available controls (with the VBX extension). For more information about additional controls, consult Appendix B.

The *Open Project* command from the *File* menu (Alt-F,
O) provides a list of all files which belong to a particular
project. Select the *All Files (*.*)* option from the *List
Files of Type* list. Two files belong to our project:
ICON_TV.FRM and ICON_TV.MAK.

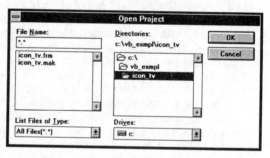

Quit the dialog window by clicking on *Cancel*.

1.8 ICON_TV, printing the program listings

Black on white

A program in Visual Basic is constructed out of a large number of components: objects, properties, parameters, events and procedures. In order to get a better overview of all these file components, it is advisable to print the contents of the project.

The *Print* command from the *File* menu (Alt-F,P or Ctrl-P) opens the Print dialog window.

By clicking on the square check boxes, you can specify which data you wish to have printed. Activate at least one of the options. We advise you to activate all three options (*Form, Form Text* and *Code*) for the examples in this book.

Note: The *Form Text* option generates a list of the properties of the form and of the controls contained in the form.

The option buttons in this dialog window determine whether only the current form is printed or the entire project. Click on the *OK* button to begin the printing process. We presume that your printer is correctly installed in Windows.

1.9   Requesting help

When working with Visual Basic you will undoubtedly arrive at a point where you wish to obtain more information. In that case, open the *Help* menu and select the *Contents* option (Alt-H, C). The first help window is opened.

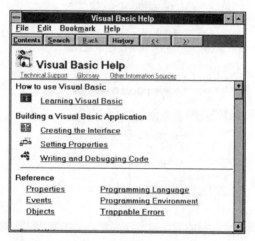

The most informative part of this window is the *Reference* section. Here, information is grouped into the categories *Properties, Events, Objects, Programming Language, Programming Environment* and *Trappable Errors*.

We want, for instance, to obtain information about the *Left* property. Activate the *Properties* group by clicking on it. This opens a window containing an alphabetical list of all properties which can be defined in Visual Basic. Click on the *L* button in this window in order to display the properties which begin with the letter L.

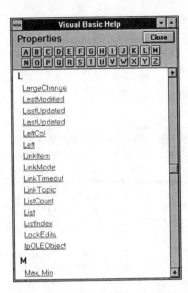

Click on the word *Left* in order to open the window containing detailed information about the *Left* property.

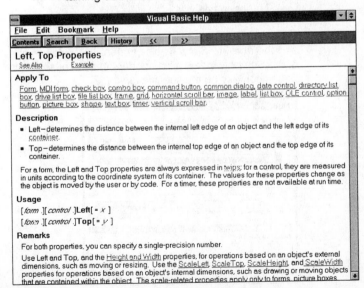

By clicking on the terms which are underlined and shown in green, you can gain information about related topics.

Context-oriented help via F1

The context-oriented help function simplifies the search procedure considerably. If a control in a form or a property in the Properties window is marked, you can obtain information relevant to that particular object by pressing the F1 key. In the code window you must first place the cursor somewhere in the name of the command about which you wish to gain more information and then press F1 to activate the corresponding help page.

If the help pages do not contain the information you are looking for, you can open the *Search* window by pressing the Alt-S key combination. Type the letters of the topic about which you require help. When you have typed the L, a list of all topics which begin with L is shown (with a scroll bar). When you have typed LE, the topic Left becomes visible.

Double click on the relevant term (or click on the term and then on the *Show Topics* button. In the lower part of the Search window a list appears of all available help pages concerning the specific topic.

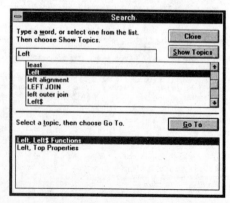

Although the help system does not always provide
exactly the required information, it does provide in general a good outline of the topics and functions available, in a clear and comprehensible manner. Accordingly, we advise you to take the time to read the help
texts when you encounter functions and topics you do
not fully understand. Time spent here is easily regained
when working more efficiently.

Exercises

1   There are two ways of placing a control in an ac-
    tive form. What are they?
    a) _____
        _____
    b) _____
        _____

2   Which control is required to display the following
    information?
    a) The currently active drive: _____
    b) The directory list: _____
    c) The currently active filenames: _____

3   Which properties define the screen position of a
    control and its size?
    _____
    _____

4   What does the unit of measurement *twip* describe,
    and how many twip is 2.5 inches?
    _____
    _____

5   Which property and which value can be defined so
    that the size of the form cannot be altered and that
    the border consists of a thick coloured line?
    _____

6   What is the difference in function between the *Caption* property and the *Name* property in a form?

_____

_____

7   Which effect does the *TabIndex* property have?

_____

_____

8   When working in the code window, you can add or modify program lines. When you leave a line, Visual Basic will indicate that there is an error if something is not correct. How does it do this?

a) _____

b) _____

9   What is an event procedure?

_____

_____

Answers

1   There are two ways of placing a control in an active form. What are they?
a) Double click on the icon in the toolbox.
b) Click on the icon in the toolbox, and drag it open in the form window.

2   Which control is required to display the following information?
a) The currently active drive: Drive list box
b) The directory list: Directory list box
c) The currently active filenames: File list box.

3   Which properties define the screen position of a control and its size?

Left and *Top* are the co-ordinates of the upper left-hand corner.

Height defines the height and *Width* the width.

4   What does the unit of measurement *twip* describe, and how many twip is 2.5 inches?

The twip is the logical unit of distance measurement in Visual Basic.

1440 twip is 1 inch, therefore 2.5 inches is 3600 twip.

5   Which property and which value can be defined so that the size of the form cannot be altered and that the border consists of a thick coloured line?

The property *BorderStyle* = 3.

6   What is the difference in function between the *Caption* property and the *Name* property in a form?

The *Caption* property contains the text which is displayed in the title bar of the form.

The *Name* property is the name by which the form and its properties can be addressed.

7   Which effect does the *TabIndex* property have?

The *TabIndex* property defines the order of sequence in which the controls can be activated by means of the Tab key.

8   When working in the code window, you can add or modify program lines. When you leave a line, Visual Basic will indicate that there is an error if something is not correct. How does it do this?
   a) A serious error will be indicated by an error message which refers to the syntax.
   b) The colour of the command or function name does *not* change from black to blue as it should.

9   What is an event procedure?

An event procedure is an independent routine
whose code is executed when a certain event occurs which is linked to this code. For example: a
click on a command button causes the Click event.

2 The ICONLIST project

The ICONLIST project is based on the result of the ICON_TV project. Therefore, we shall copy the ICON_TV project file under a new name, ICONLIST, to the VB_EXMPL\ICONLIST directory. The name ICON_TV remains the same.

Note: If you wish to use an existing project as the basis for a new project, it is advisable to let Visual Basic do the copying. This ensures that all the necessary files will be copied.

In our example, the procedure is as follows:

1   Load the ICON_TV.MAK project by selecting *Open Project* from the *File* menu. Double click on ICON_TV in the directories list. Click on ICON_TV.MAK in the file list box and then on *OK*. If the ICON_TV.MAK window does not appear on your screen immediately, Open the *Window* menu and click on *Project.* .

2   Open the ICON_TV.FRM form window by double clicking on ICON_TV.FRM IconTV in the subsequent window.

3   Select *Save File As* from the *File* menu (Alt-F, A or Ctrl-A).

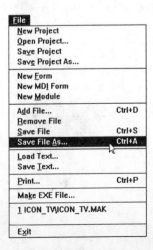

4   Switch to the C:\VB_EXMPL\ICONLIST directory
     by double clicking on VB_EXMPL to produce the
     list of subdirectories. Then double click on ICON-
     LIST.
5   Confirm the old name, ICON_TV.FRM which is still
     in the File Name box by clicking on *OK*.
6   Save the ICON_TV.MAK project file in the same
     way by selecting *Save Project As* from the *File*
     menu (Alt-F, E).
     Save it in the directory C:\VB_EXMPL\ICONLIST
     under the new name ICONLIST.MAK.
7   Open the new project ICONLIST.MAK by selecting
     Open Project from the *File* menu (Alt-F,O) and ac-
     tivating the name.

We have now completed all the preparation necessary
to be able to begin the ICONLIST project.

2.1   ICONLIST, the project description

The ICON_TV program which we created in the previous chapter shows one icon at a time. This means that
it is quite laborious to have to look through a whole series of files when you are searching for one specific
icon. Our ICONLIST program is going to add a form to
the ICON_TV window, which will display all the icons in
a directory. The new window will be opened from the
ICON_TV window by means of a command button.

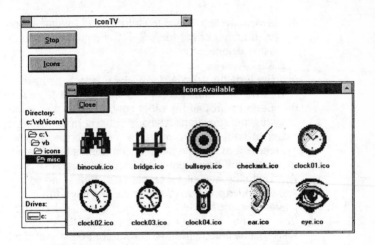

2.2 ICONLIST, creating the work area

The IconTV form (ICON_TV.FRM)

Using the toolbox, place a second command button under the *Stop* button in the IconTV form; this button is given the default name Command1 just as its predecessor. This new button will be used to open the window displaying the icons.

The new form, IconList (ICONLIST.FRM)

In order to display the icons, we shall make a separate form. Generate this form by clicking on the button at the extreme left-hand side of the toolbar or by selecting *New Project* from the *File* menu (Alt-F, N). The new form is assigned the working name Form1 for the time being.

Place a command button (Command1) in the upper left-hand corner of the form. This button will be used to close the window.

Just as with the IconTV form, each icon is to be displayed along with its filename. Using the toolbox, place an Image control and a Label control in the new form. Only one Image control and one Label control are to be made at first. We only need to create these controls once in order to define the basic properties for *all* registrations in the list of icon files, in other words the position and size etc. of these controls. Since we do not know in advance how many icons will have to be displayed, the list has to be managed dynamically. To do this, we shall place a command block in the program; this block will copy the two output controls a sufficient number of times.

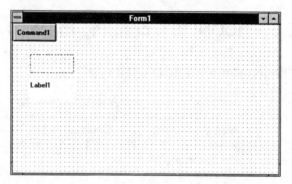

2.3   ICONLIST, defining the properties

The new controls in the two forms will be assigned the properties shown on the next page. First open the ICON_TV.FRM form window by double clicking on this name in the project window. The form window appears. Click on the Command1 control to activate it. Open the *Window* menu and click on *Properties*. Now modify the properties as shown on the next page by clicking on them in turn:

Command1 CommandButton
Caption	= &Icons
Height	= 465
Left	= 180
Name	= IconRegister
TabIndex	= 5
Top	= 720
Width	= 1365

The ICONLIST form

Because the ICONLIST.FRM form (IconList, currently still Form1) which is going to display the icons is dependent on the IconTV form, IconList always has to be closed before the program can return to IconTV.

The *MinButton=False* property prevents the possibility of reducing the IconList form window to an icon.

Open the Projects window and double click on Form1.frm. Now open the Properties window (*Window* menu, *Properties*). Change the properties as shown below:

Form1 Form
Caption	= IconsAvailable
Height	= 4305
Left	= 1230
Minbutton	= False
Name	= IconList
Top	= 1635
Width	= 8295

Command1 CommandButton
Caption	= &Close
Height	= 465
Left	= 0
Name	= IconListClose
TabIndex	= 0
Top	= 0
Width	= 1185

Image1 Image
Height	= 915
Left	= 360
Name	= ImageList
Stretch	= True
Top	= 810
Width	= 915

Label1 Label
Alignment	= 2 - Center
Caption	=
Height	= 195
Left	= 90
Name	= IconFileList
Top	= 1890
Width	= 1500

2.4   ICONLIST, writing the program code

We shall first write the program code for the *Icons* command button in the IconTV form. This procedure will enable or prevent the activation of the IconList form.

Switch to the IconTV form and activate the code window. Open the Object list and select the internal name IconSwitch which we assigned to the *Icons* command button.

In our project, the procedure must first of all examine whether or not there are any icon files in the current directory. The *ListCount* property contains information as to whether there are registrations in a list of files (File1 control) and if so, how many.

The If-Then-Else operating structure

A program can make a choice out of two options; the choice is based on a condition (comparison) in the If section of the *If-Then-Else* operating structure. If the condition is fulfilled (thus if the comparison is met), the Then section is executed. If not (thus in all other cases), the Else section is executed. The branched construction ends with a line which contains only the *End If* command.

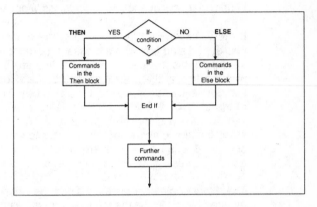

This If-Then-Else structure is well-known in everyday life:

If I win the pools, then I'll go to the Bahamas. If not, I'll have to work till I'm 65.
End IF

If the value of File1.ListCount is greater than zero, there is at least one icon file. (The symbol > means 'greater than', the symbol < means 'smaller than' and the combination <> means 'not equal to'.) In that case, the condition for switching to the IconList form has been fulfilled. The window is loaded and opened via the *Show* method; the method parameter indicates the mode as long as the window is open:

1   *Modal:* commands given after the *Show* instruction are only executed when the window has been closed again; prior to this, it is not possible to give input via another form.

0   *Modeless:* the program continues immediately with
      the next command given, for example the reaction
      to clicking on a button in another window.

A modal window must be closed before the program
can continue working in the form at a higher level. This
condition does not apply to a modeless window.

If the value of File1.Count is zero, the routine should
display a dialog box with a message (a message box).
To create this message we shall define an FM$ string
with the text of the error message and a code for the
standardized appearance of this dialog box. The $ sign
at the end of the FM variable name indicates that this
variable has a string of the data type. The *UCase&()*
string function changes all small letters to capitals. The
sum of 48 and 0 is 48. The 0 represents the *OK* button,
and 48 represents the icon with the exclamation mark.

The *MousePointer* property defines the shape of the
mouse pointer. While the IconList form is being loaded,
the mouse pointer assumes the shape of an hour-glass
(code 11); the 0 setting restores the standard shape to
the mouse pointer (an arrow).

Add the following code (shown in bold) to the Icon-
Switch_Click routine:

```
Sub IconSwitch_Click ()
    If (File1.ListCount) > 0 Then
        MousePointer = 11
        IconSwitch.Show 1
    Else
        FM$ = "No " + UCase$(File1.Pattern) +
              " files found."
        MsgBox FM$, 48
    End If
    MousePointer = 0
End Sub
```

Remember that in this book, input which should be

placed on one program line is shown behind the ⟳ symbol.

Start the program by pressing the F5 function key and click on the *Icons* button. If everything has gone as it should, the dialog box with the error message should appear. Acknowledge the message by clicking on *OK* and switch to a directory which does contain icons. Click on the *Icons* button to activate the list. Only the *Close* button is shown in the subsequent window. Because the event procedure for *Close* still has to be written, we shall end the program by selecting *End* from the *Run* menu.

In the Project window, activate the code window of the IconList window (ICONLIST.FRM). We shall close this modal window by applying the *Unload* procedure when the command button (which has been given the name IconListClose) is activated.

```
Sub IconListClose_Click ()
     Unload IconList
End Sub
```

Loading the icons in the display form

We shall presume that the current directory contains icon files. The problem we are now facing is how to display the icons along with their filenames in the IconList window. The filenames must be conveyed from the IconTV form to the IconList form. This is possible by means of global variables.

Global variables

Within a project, a form is an independent unit. No data can be exchanged between two forms because the forms contain only local variables. Therefore, we shall declare *global variables* which will be valid for both forms.

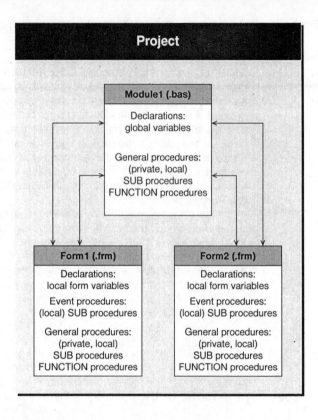

Managing elements by means of an index

In order to be able to open a file, we need to know the full pathname and filename. Since a directory usually contains more than one file, we would really require a variable for each filename in order to save the data, for example: FileA, FileB, ..., FileZZZ. Since this would be very laborious when programming, we shall make use of the possibility of managing a *list* of various values by means of one variable name. This type of list of similar variables is called an *array*. The values are distinguished from one another by a consecutive number, such as File(0), File(1), ..., File(999). This consecutive number is called the *index*. In our example, the index begins at the value 0.

Since the directory contains a limited number of file-names, it is useful to determine this in advance for management purposes. If we did not do this, we would continually have to check whether or not the end of the list had been reached.

Thus, we need three global variables:

■ Route1$: the string with the current directory path
■ Fylename(Index)
■ FNameNr: the number of icon files in the current directory.

Note: We shall use Route as the name of the first variable to represent the path; Path itself is a reserved word in the programming language. For the same reason we shall use Fylename instead of Filename for the second variable.

The global variables are managed in a separate module. We generate this module by means of the *New Module* command from the *File* menu (Alt-F, M). A new code window with the name Module1.bas then appears on the screen. In our project we shall use this module under the name GLOBAL1.BAS. Accordingly, change the default name using the *Save File As* option from the *File* menu (Alt-F, A or Ctrl-A) and type the following commands in the code window:

```
Global Route1$
Global Fylename(0 To 255)
Global FNameNr As Integer
```

The *Global* command declares a variable as a *global variable*. The information concerning the drive and directory path are stored as a string in the *Route1$* variable.

In the case of a variable with an index (an *array*), the interval between the lowest and highest valid index value, divided by the word *To*, is shown between brackets. The value shown here, 255, is a random value. The lower and upper limits of the *Integer* type are respectively -32,768 and 32,767 in Visual Basic. We shall use 0 for the first filename, which means that the largest amount of icon files which can be managed and displayed in the icon list is 256. Because the amount of memory occupied by an index variable increases according to the index interval, the upper limit should not be too large. An index is always a whole number.

Note: The Help function provides information about all Visual Basic data types under the topic *data types*.

We shall need the number of filenames later in the program for the index management of the filenames. The *FNameNr* variable is a whole number; the annex *As Integer* declares that the value of this data type is an integer, in other words, a whole number.

The Project window now indicates that the GLO-BAL1.BAS module is now a component of the project list.

Making the filenames globally accessible

The Dir1_Change procedure is executed at each directory switch. If we add the new code here, we know that the currently active filename will always be globally available. We shall copy the pathname from the local *File1.Path* variable to the *Route1$* global variable, and the number of valid filenames to the *FNameNr* global variable.

These actions are only useful if there really are files which fulfil the conditions. Accordingly, we shall check in advance whether or not the number of registrations is greater than zero. In this case, the Else branch of the operating structure becomes redundant because the program may only react to a positive value resulting from the comparison. In that case, the local list of filenames is conveyed to the global file list.

The For-Next operating structure

The number of filenames is accessible and available in the *ListCount* property. A loop structure enables the list of files to be copied by means of a single command. Because the number of elements in the array is already known before the start of the loop, it is obvious that a loop with a counting structure of the type For-Next should be used. This structure consists of an opening line, a command block and a closing line:

For *Counter=Beginvalue* To *Endvalue*
    Command block
Next *Counter*

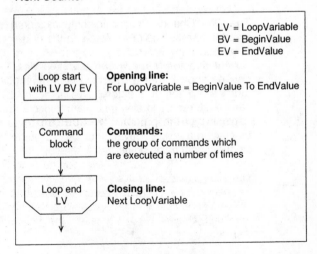

LV = LoopVariable
BV = BeginValue
EV = EndValue

Loop start with LV BV EV

Opening line:
For LoopVariable = BeginValue To EndValue

Command block

Commands:
the group of commands which are executed a number of times

Loop end LV

Closing line:
Next LoopVariable

The counting loop runs via the Index counter through the values 0 to the number of files minus one. The index of the first file is 0, not 1. In other words, the last file in the array has an index number which is one less than the total number of (valid) files. For 50 files for instance, the index runs from 0 to 49.

Extend the Dir1_Change routine (in ICON_TV.FRM) by adding the lines shown in boldface below:

```
Sub Dir1_Change ()
    File1.Path = Dir1.Path
    Route1$ = File1.Path
    FNameNr = File1.ListCount
    Way.Caption = Dir1.Path
    If File1.ListCount > 0 Then
        For Index = 0 To File1.ListCount - 1
            Fylename(Index) = File1.List(Index)
        Next Index
    End If
    File.Caption = ""
    Imidge.Picture = LoadPicture()
End Sub
```

The Dir1_Change routine is only executed when a switch of directories takes place. In the present version of our program, if, when the program is started up, the current directory already contains icon files, they can only be shown after a Change event, thus after a detour via a different directory. This is inconvenient and can be altered by forcing this event to occur right at the beginning of the program (in the Form_Load routine) by placing a 'false' activation of Dir1_Change to initialize the global filename list.

```
Sub Form_Load ()
    Way.Caption = Dir1.Path
    File1.Pattern = "*.ico"
    Dir1_Change
End Sub
```

The icon files

The valid filenames are now available in the *Fylename(Index)* array variable from the start of the program. This list will be used as the basis to display the icons along with the filenames in the IconList form. We have already defined the controls for this output: the ImageList and IconFileList controls respectively.

The next stage in the program is to copy the two original elements as often as the number of registrations in the *FNameNr* global variable and to save them in two arrays with controls, thus two collections of a given number of similar controls. The copies of the original control inherit the properties of that control. The original controls themselves may not be displayed because their function is purely to serve as originals to be copied.

The *Visible* property enables us to specify whether or not a control is to be visible during the execution of the program (True or False). Change the *Visible* property to False (thus the control will not be shown) for the ImageList and IconFileList controls (in the IconList form).

ImageList Image
Visible = False

IconFileList Label
Visible = False

The copies of the controls will be made by giving the *Index* property an increasing number; this property is a whole number which may have a value between 0 and 32,767. We shall assign the original controls the index 0 and an index ranging from 1 to 255 to the controls which are to be dynamically displayed later.

Switch to the code window of the ImageList control. You will see that the space between the two brackets in the top line is empty.

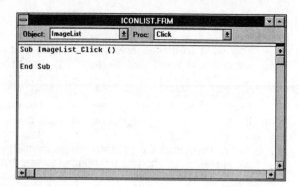

Switch to the properties window and assign the value 0
to the *Index* property of the ImageList and IconFileList
controls.

ImageList Image
Index = 0

IconFileList Label
Index = 0

If you now examine the code window of the ImageList
control once more, you will see that the annex (Index
as Integer) has been placed between the brackets automatically.

Loading, displaying and removing icons

The display of an icon takes place in three phases.
Firstly, by means of the Form_Load procedure, we load
into memory all icons and their filenames as elements
of the controls array. In the second phase, the icons

are shown in the IconList form by means of the self-defined Windows_Fill general procedure. Finally, the contents of all controls are removed. We shall add these commands to the IconListClose control.

The various controls are managed in *stack* form. The stack is filled from below when it is loaded, which means the last element is placed on top. When displaying an element and when clearing the stack, the management procedure begins with the element which was last saved. Since the first element should be displayed first on the screen, we shall ensure that the first element is placed at the top of the stack and the last element at the bottom. This is done by making the loop count backwards during the loading routine, from high to low.

When switching to the IconList form, the Form_Load event takes place automatically. The loop with the Index counter loads the ImageList and IconFileList controls in memory for each index number. The LoadPicture function assigns the *Picture* property to the ImageList display element. The argument for this function is the full name: a combined string consisting of the path plus the filename. The *Index* variable should be decreased by 1 because the filenames are counted from 0 onwards, but the icon display should begin at 1. The filename is to be placed in the *Caption* property of the IconFileList label box. Here too we must remember that the numbering of the indexes differs by one.

The top line of the loop will indicate that the loop is counting backwards. We determine this by placing the *Step* parameter behind the ultimate counter value along with the value -1. If you do not specify this, the default step size is +1. By reversing the order of sequence, we ensure that the icons are shown onscreen corresponding to index number.

The Windows_Fill command activates a general procedure which operates the display of icons and filenames. We still have to develop and code this procedure.

We shall now first write the Form_Load routine for the IconList form:

```
Sub Form_Load ()
    MousePointer = 11
        For Index = FNameNr To 1 Step -1
            Load ImageList(Index)
            ImageList(Index).Picture =
↺               LoadPicture(Route1$ + "\" +
↺               Fylename(Index - 1))
            Load IconFileList(Index)
            IconFileList(Index).Caption =
↺               Fylename(Index - 1)
        Next Index
    MousePointer = 0
    Windows_Fill
End Sub
```

Remember that the lines preceded here by arrows should be placed on the previous line in the actual program.

The Windows_Fill general object

Although the Windows_Fill routine can also be added to a control, we wish to make it a *general procedure*. This has the advantage that the routine can also be activated from another routine, thus without having to link the Windows_Fill routine to a fixed event. In this way, you can avoid the necessity of having to repeatedly code a routine which recurs with different events at various places in the program. Since we shall have to deal with that in the further extension of the example, we shall apply this technique now.

A general procedure is created by means of the *New Procedure* option from the *View* menu (Alt-V, N). This can only be done if the code window is active. Type the name Windows_Fill in the Name box of the dialog window and conclude the input by clicking on *OK*.

This object is now displayed in the Object options list in the code window under the *(general)* registration. The specific routine is included in the *Proc* options list.

In our project we have now reached the stage in which the icons are available in memory and are accessible via their filename. The *Visible=False* property prevents the display. In order to make them visible we only have to change the value of this property during the loop to True.

Type the following code in the Windows_Fill routine and try out the result:

```
Sub Windows_Fill ()
MousePointer = 11
    For Index = 1 To FNameNr
        ImageList(Index).Visible = True
        IconFileList(Index).Visible = True
    Next Index
MousePointer = 0
End Sub
```

As you see, this is not quite what we intend. Instead of a series of icons being placed next to one another, two small films are run in the image fields: one shows the icons and the other the filenames. It all goes too quickly to be able to judge whether everything has been displayed properly in conjunction. Only the last two pieces of data remain visible.

Each icon at its own position

The display area for the icons is restricted to the inner section of the IconList form (ICONLIST.FRM, IconList, with the caption IconsAvailable). The size of the section of the form window which is visible during the execution of the program is determined by means of the *ScaleHeight* and *ScaleWidth*.

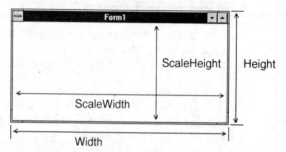

If there are many icons, there is not sufficient room to show them all on one horizontal row: the display procedure continues on the next row once the right-hand edge has been reached. This will go on until all the icons have been displayed.

We shall declare three variables for positioning the icons and their filenames in the IconList form:

■   *Grid*: the space required to display an icon and the filename in horizontal and vertical direction.
■   *PosFromLeft*: the current distance to the left-hand edge. This value is set to 50 each time for the first icon on the row.
■   *PosFromTop*: the current distance to the top edge. This value is set to 750 for the first row to prevent the first icon being displayed over the *Close* command button.

In order to centre an icon in relation to its corresponding filename, the *Left* property of the icon image should be increased by 300 twip. This can be calculated from the specified width of the ImageList (1500) and IconFileList (915) controls. The difference of roughly 600 is shared over the left- and right-hand space.

Measured from the top of the icon, the filename is always 1050 twip lower (in other words, the value of the vertical co-ordinate is higher).

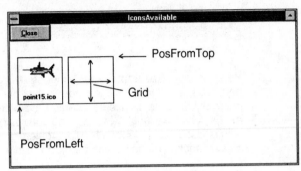

Go to the ICONLIST.FRM window and click on Windows_Fill in the Proc. list.
Complete the Windows_Fill procedure as follows:

```
Sub Windows_Fill ()
MousePointer = 11

    Grid = 1500
    PosFromLeft = 50
    PosFromTop = 750


For Index = 1 To FNameNr
    ImageList(Index).Left = PosFromLeft + 300
    ImageList(Index).Top = PosFromTop
    ImageList(Index).Visible = True
    IconFileList(Index).Left = PosFromLeft
    IconFileList(Index).Top = PosFromTop + 1050
    IconFileList(Index).Visible = True


    If (PosFromLeft + Grid +
            IconFileList(Index).Width)
            > IconList.ScaleWidth Then
        PosFromLeft = 50
        PosFromTop = PosFromTop + Grid
```

```
        Else
              PosFromLeft = PosFromLeft + Grid
        End If
   Next Index

MousePointer = 0
End Sub
```

You will now see that larger amounts of icons are
neatly displayed in rows but unfortunately the third row
is largely invisible, concealed behind the bottom edge
of the IconsAvailable window. The following chapter
discusses how to deal with this problem and how a
chosen section of the list can be made visible.

2.5   Examining the program and recti-
fying errors

Before proceeding further with this chapter, we recommend you to study the *Debugging Your Application* lesson in the *Help* menu of the *Learning Microsoft Visual
Basic* program.

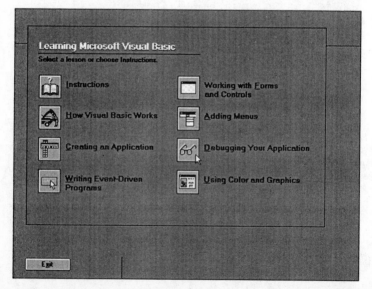

We shall explain the monitoring of the program by examining how the counter in a loop changes during the execution of a program. As an example, we shall study the Index counter which regulates the structure of the icon list. This counter is applied in the Windows_Fill routine, a general procedure in the IconList form.

Open the code window of the Windows_Fill routine, mark the word *Index* behind the command *For* by double clicking on it and open the *Debug* menu.

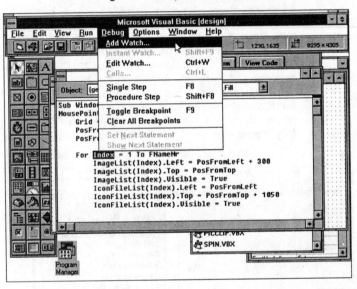

The *Add Watch* command opens a dialog window in which the marked variable, in this case Index, is shown as an *Expression* which is to be followed in the current procedure. Confirm the contents of this window by clicking on *OK*.

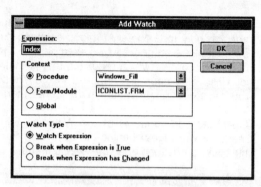

Now close all Visual Basic windows except the Design window and the Project window. Run the program by pressing F5. The Debug window appears in the lower right-hand corner. If this is partially hidden, click on the title bar to bring it to the foreground. Shift the IconTV window to the left as far as possible and widen the Debug window so that the line under the title bar becomes fully legible.

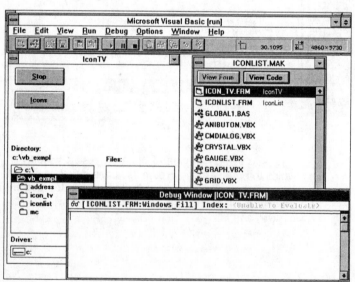

It appears as if nothing has changed in the Debug window during the runthrough of the program. Concerning *Index*, Visual Basic can only state in light grey letters *Unable To Evaluate*. The value of *Index* however has been followed, but that happened so rapidly that there was no time to display it. If we want to see this, we must ensure that the execution of the program is interrupted each time the *Index* variable is altered.

End the ICON_TV program and give the command *Edit Watch* from the *Debug* menu (Alt-D, E or Ctrl-W). Click on the *Edit* button in the subsequent dialog box. A window now appears which we have already seen with *Add Watch*. This now has the function of enabling you to change previously specified settings. In the *Watch Type* section of this window, activate the *Break when Expression has Changed* option. Close the two dialog windows by means of *OK* and *Close* respectively. Now start the ICON_TV program again. Click on the Icons button to activate the display and thus the *Index* counter.

When the icon list is loaded, the *Index* counter is increased. The program, as instructed, now interrupts this process. The text box in the *Debug* window now shows *Index: 1*. In addition, the code window of the routine in question (Windows_Fill) has been opened and the line which follows the command causing the change is marked by a frame. The cursor is positioned at the beginning of this line.

You can now run through the program step by step by pressing F8. If you hold down the F8 key, the program will run. Each time the loop is executed the value of *Index* is increased by 1 until the IconList window (with the title IconsAvailable which we specified as caption) appears on the screen. The *Index* variable does not occur in the program any more after this. The text box in the *Debug* window now shows *Index: <Not In Context>*. End the program and remove the marked topic in the *Edit Watch* window (*Debug* menu) by activating the *Delete (All)* button. Then click on *Close*.

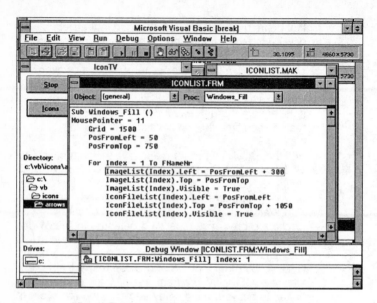

Visual Basic provides many more and also more pow-
erful facilities for analysing a program than we can
demonstrate within the scope of this book. In addition,
the method of control depends on what exactly you
wish to examine. In fact the best practical method is to
look for errors in the programs which you write yourself.

Exercises

1   What is the difference between local and global
    variables?

    _____

    _____

2   Describe the data types:
    a) Integer: _____
    b) String: _____

3   In which way can you use one variable name to
    manage various values simultaneously?

    _____

4   At which points in a program is it useful to apply
    the For-Next loop structure?

_____

5   Which logical structure is used to determine
    whether a program should execute either one pro-
    gram block or another?

_____

Answers

1   What is the difference between local and global
    variables?
    Global variables are accessible within the entire
    project. Local variables are only available within
    one form or even only within one routine.

2   Describe the data types:
    a) Integer: all whole numbers between -32,768
       and +32 767 inclusive.
    b) String: a series of characters with a maximum
       length of 65,535 bytes, not counting the code
       symbols (inverted commas) at the beginning
       and end.

3   In which way can you use one variable name to
    manage various values simultaneously?

    The variable receives an index and the individual
    values are assigned an increasing consecutive
    number. The whole is called an array.

4   At which points in a program is it useful to apply
    the For-Next loop structure?

    At those points where the number of times that a
    loop is to be executed is known in advance and
    where the index counter of the variable used to ex-
    ecute the action can be used.

5   Which logical structure is used to determine
     whether a program should execute either one pro-
     gram block or another?

     The branch structure If-Then-Else makes it possi-
     ble to execute different blocks, based on the result
     of a comparison or condition.

3 The ICONLIST II project

3.1 ICONLIST II, the project description

The current version of the program we have just created displays an overview of the icon files in the current directory. This overview does not take the number of files into account: the icons are shown to the extent allowed by the size of the window. In cases where there are larger amounts of files, we wish to include the possibility of using a scroll bar to browse forwards and backwards through the icons. In addition, we shall extend the window with a status line which indicates the total number of icons available and also the list numbers of the icons shown.

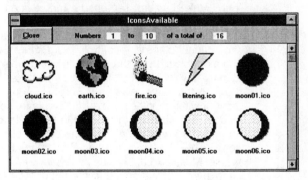

3.2 ICONLIST II, extending the work area

We shall change the work area so that the various functions of each section can be distinguished more easily. We shall create a status line along the top of the window which will show, in addition to explanatory text, the numbers of the icons shown in the upper left-hand corner and the lower right-hand corner. The status line will also indicate the number of icon files in the current directory. The *Close* command button will be shifted to the status line.

Only the Picture Box control is suited to being used for the status line, since this control is the only one with the *Align* property. This property automatically adjusts the width of the control to the width of the form. In addition, you can specify whether the line is to be placed at the top, in the middle or at the bottom of the form.

A Picture Box, just like a form, may contain various controls; they then form a logical unit with the Picture Box. This means that when the Picture box is moved, these controls are moved along with it.

Place a Picture Box control in the IconList form (ICON-LIST.FRM with the caption IconsAvailable in the title bar). Make it wider, but ensure that it does not cover the *Close* button.

You cannot place any controls in a Picture Box by giving a double click on the control. If you double click on a control, it will be placed in the form just like the Picture box, on the same level as it were. In order to place a control within another control (thus a level deeper) this is done by activating the control in the toolbox and then dragging a frame open within the control already in the form. The chosen control is then placed within this frame. Make six Label fields for display in the status line in this way. Leave space in the upper left-hand corner for the *Close* button which will be placed here.

In order to adopt the *Close* box into the Picture Box, we shall copy it from the form via the Clipboard:

1   Activate the *Close* button by clicking on it.
2   Remove the button by clicking on *Cut* in the *Edit* menu (Alt-E, T or Ctrl-X).
3   Activate the Picture Box by clicking on it.
4   Adopt the *Close* button into the Picture Box by clicking on *Paste* in the *Edit* menu (Alt-E, P or Ctrl-V).
5   If necessary, move the *Close* button to the extreme left-hand side of the status line.

In order to browse through the overview of icons, we shall require a scroll bar. Click on the Vertical Scroll Bar control in the toolbox and then place it in the Icon-List form.

3.3   ICONLIST II, defining the properties

Change the properties of the new controls to the values shown below.

Picture1 PictureBox
Align	= 1 - Align Top
BackColor	= &H00C0C0C0& (light grey)
	(can also be done by double click-ing and then clicking on light grey)
Height	= 495
Name	= TopLine
TabStop	= False

The *TabStop=False* property prevents the Picture Box being activated by the Tab key: this control must not be able to be activated later by the program user.

Label1 Label
Alignment	= 2 - Center
Caption	=
Height	= 195
Left	= 2700
Name	= FirstOut
Top	= 165
Width	= 375

Label2 Label
Alignment	= 2 - Center
Caption	=
Height	= 195
Left	= 3690
Name	= LastOut
Top	= 165
Width	= 375

Label3 Label
Alignment   = 2 - Center
Caption   =
Height   = 195
Left   = 5670
Name   = FNumOut
Top   = 165
Width   = 375

Label4 Label
BackColor   = &H00C0C0C0& (light grey)
Caption   = Numbers
Height   = 195
Left   = 1800
Top   = 150
Width   = 800

Label5 Label
Alignment   = 2 - Center
BackColor   = &H00C0C0C0& (light grey)
Caption   = to
Height   = 195
Left   = 3240
Top   = 150
Width   = 285

Label6 Label
Alignment   = 2 - Center
BackColor   = &H00C0C0C0& (light grey)
Caption   = of a total of
Height   = 195
Left   = 4230
Top   = 150
Width   = 1275

IconListClose1 CommandButton
TabIndex   = 1

The properties of the scroll bar

VScroll1 VScrollBar
Enabled   = False
Height   = 3195
Left   = 7830
Min   = 1
Name   = VertScroll
TabIndex   = 2
Top   = 630

The scroll bar (VertScroll) should only be visible when there are too many icons in the current directory to be displayed in the visible part of the form. Accordingly, we shall change the default setting of the *Enabled* property to False. We shall write the code for this control in such a way that the scroll bar is only displayed when it is necessary to make another section of the remaining icons visible.

A scroll bar has various properties whose values may range from -32,768 to 32,767. The limits of the values which can be defined by means of the scroll bar are *Min* and *Max*. The current value, which of course lies between these, is *Value*. The size of the interval changes produced by one mouse click are *Large-Change* (a click in front or behind the scroll block) and *SmallChange* (a click on the arrow). We shall use the *SmallChange* property to scroll the icon overview an interval of one row; we shall use *LargeChange* to scroll the icon overview one window page.

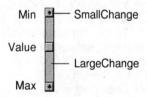

We shall give the *Min* property the value 1 because the first element in the index management has the number

1. The value of the *Value* property, which depends on the position of the scroll block, is automatically adjusted to this new value of the *Min* property.

3.4   ICONLIST II, extending the program code

We shall adjust the icon display to the size of the display window. In addition, if there are more icons than fit into the form window, the portion of icons currently being displayed must be able to be altered (browsing, scrolling). In order to display the icons in an orderly way, we shall divide the list of icons into sections which fit onto the rows in the current window. The number of icons on each row and the number of rows displayed depend on the current window measurements. The form then becomes a kind of hatch or port-hole which is moved up and down over the rows of icons.

Managing the display in the display window

The program will regulate the operation of the icon display in the display window. We shall extend the Windows_Fill procedure by adding a number of commands.

We determine the contents of the visible part of the icon list by means of three variables:

1   *BValue*: the begin value (the index of the icon in the upper left-hand corner). The variable is an index number and therefore the value must be a whole number. This is not automatically the case when a variable first appears in a program. Accordingly, the command *Dim BValue As Integer* must be placed in the ICONLIST.FRM code window. Type this command in the (still blank) code window under Object: (general).

2   *EValue*: the end value (the index of the icon in the lower right-hand corner).

3   *FNameNr*, the number of icon files already specified.

The *IconsPerRow* variable contains the number of icons which can be fitted onto one row. This value is calculated by taking the width of the IconList form, subtracting 50 twip from the left-hand side and reserving space for the scroll bar at the right-hand side. The result is divided by *Grid*, the size of the rectangular display area.

The *IconRows* variable contains the number of rows of icons which can be displayed. This number is obtained by taking the height of the form, subtracting the height of the status line (750 twip) and dividing the result by the grid size.

In order to know, in the program, whether or not the visible area is full, we shall declare the *WindowFull* variable whose value is equal to the product of *IconsPerRow* and *IconRows*.

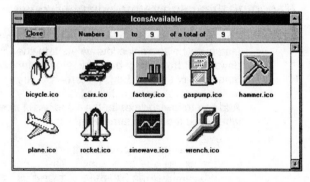

Type the lines shown on the next page in boldface in the first part of the program code of the Windows_Fill general object.

```
Sub Windows_Fill ()
MousePointer = 11

    Grid = 1500
    PosFromLeft = 50
    PosFromTop = 750

    IconsPerRow = Int((IconList.ScaleWidth -
↺       50 - VertScroll.Width) / Grid)
    IconRows = Int((IconList.ScaleHeight - 750)
↺       / Grid)
    WindowFull = IconsPerRow * IconRows
```

The test which indicates whether or not the window is
to be filled with a new set of icons consists of a number
of conditions. Here we must distinguish between two
instances:

1   Overviews of icons which completely fit into the
     display window.
2   Larger overviews of icons which require more
     room than the display window provides.

The first If-Then block distinguishes between these two
instances by assigning the value 1 to the initial value
(BValue) if the icon overview is small; in that case, the
scroll bar is switched off. If there is a large icon overview, the scroll bar is activated.
Add the following lines to the Windows_Fill subroutine
where you left off a moment ago:

```
    If FNameNr <= WindowFull Then
        BValue = 1
        VertScroll.Enabled = False
    Else
        VertScroll.Enabled = True
    End If
```

Based on the *BValue* variable (the index of the first
icon), the value of *EValue* (the index of the last icon
that fits into the display window) has to be calculated.
We add the number of icons that fit into the window to

the current value of *BValue* and then we subtract 1 (for
the initial value of *BValue*).

```
EValue = BValue + (WindowFull - 1)
```

This newly calculated value can be smaller than, equal
to or larger than *FNameNr*. In the first two cases, the
rest of the icons will fit into the display window. If the
calculated value is larger than *FNameNr*, *EValue* will
be set to the maximum value (*FNameNr*).

```
If EValue > FNameNr Then
     EValue = FNameNr
End If
```

In order to ensure that at the end of the list the display
window remains full and that the last row does not also
shift upwards, the value of the *VertScroll* property has
to be adjusted where necessary.

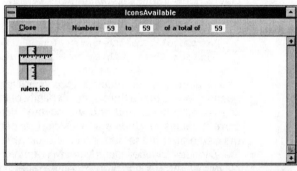

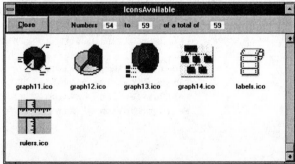

If the difference between the current starting index (*BValue*) and the total number of icons (*FNameNr*) is not sufficient to fill the whole window, the *Vert-Scroll.Max* property is assigned the value of *BValue*, which prevents any further scrolling. In all other cases, *VertScroll* is equal to the total number of icons.

```
If (FNameNr - BValue) < WindowFull Then
    VertScroll.Max = BValue
Else
    VertScroll.Max = FNameNr
End If
```

The next two commands deal with the operation of the mouse. One click on one of the arrows in the scroll bar must shift the window contents one row in the appropriate direction by means of the *SmallChange* property. One click on the area between the arrows and the scroll block must shift the window contents a whole display window in the appropriate direction by means of the *LargeChange* property.

```
VertScroll.SmallChange =  IconsPerRow
VertScroll.LargeChange =  WindowFull
```

The execution of the counter loop (For-Next) subsequently only refers to the current capacity of the display window: the begin and end values are therefore the current values of *BValue* and *EValue* respectively. At the same time in the status line, the current values of the *BValue*, *EValue* and *FNameNr* variables are displayed via the *Caption* property of the label boxes.
Accordingly, the following lines must be added to the subroutine, replacing the line For Index = 1 To FileNameNr.

```
For Index = BValue To EValue
    FirstOut.Caption = BValue
    LastOut.Caption = EValue
    FNumOut.Caption = FNameNr
```

The entire coding for the Windows_Fill procedure is
now as follows:

```
Sub Windows_Fill ()
MousePointer = 11
    Grid = 1500
    PosFromLeft = 50
    PosFromTop = 750

    IconsPerRow = Int((IconList.ScaleWidth -
↻          50 - VertScroll.Width) / Grid)
    IconRows = Int((IconList.ScaleHeight - 750)
↻          / Grid)
    WindowFull = IconsPerRow * IconRows

    If FNameNr <= WindowFull Then
        BValue = 1
        VertScroll.Enabled = False
    Else
        VertScroll.Enabled = True
    End If

    EValue = BValue + (WindowFull - 1)

    If EValue > FNameNr Then
        EValue = FNameNr
    End If

    If (FNameNr - BValue) < WindowFull Then
        VertScroll.Max = BValue
    Else
        VertScroll.Max = FNameNr
    End If

    VertScroll.SmallChange =  IconsPerRow
    VertScroll.LargeChange =  WindowFull

    For Index = BValue To EValue
        FirstOut.Caption = BValue
        LastOut.Caption = EValue
        FNumOut.Caption = FNameNr
```

```
                ImageList(Index).Left = PosFromLeft + 300
                ImageList(Index).Top = PosFromTop
                ImageList(Index).Visible = True
                IconFileList(Index).Left = PosFromLeft
                IconFileList(Index).Top = PosFromTop + 1050
                IconFileList(Index).Visible = True

                If (PosFromLeft + Grid +
↻                   IconFileList(Index).Width)
↻                   > IconList.ScaleWidth Then
                    PosFromLeft = 50
                    PosFromTop = PosFromTop + Grid
                Else
                    PosFromLeft = PosFromLeft + Grid
                End If

        Next Index
    MousePointer = 0
    End Sub
```

When the Windows_Fill procedure is activated for the
first time in the IconList form, *BValue* has to be initial-
ised with the value 1. This results in the current display
window always showing, as standard, the icons from
the beginning of the icon list onwards. The management of the window contents and the scrolling function
is regulated by the rest of the program.

```
Sub Form_Load ()
    MousePointer = 11
        For Index = FNameNr To Step -1
            Load ImageList(Index)
            ImageList(Index).Picture
↻               = LoadPicture(Route1$ + "\" +
↻               Fylename(Index -1))
            Load IconFileList(Index)
            IconFileList(Index).Caption =
↻               Fylename(Index - 1)
        Next Index
```

```
        MousePointer = 0
        BValue = 1
        Windows_Fill
End Sub
```

Each time the position of the block in the scroll bar is changed using the mouse, the Change event takes place. Then the new index of the first icon (upper left-hand corner) has to be conveyed to the *BValue* variable. In this way, we are sure that icons which correspond to that scroll block position are displayed. The *Value* property contains the value for the current position of the scroll block; this value lies between the specified limits for *Min* and *Max*. In order to display the effect of this modification in the window, the Windows_Fill general procedure has to be executed. Activate the *Proc* box and select Windows_Fill. Then select VertScroll from the *Object* box.
The code for this scroll procedure is:

```
Sub VertScroll_Change ()
        BValue = VertScroll.Value
        Windows_Fill
End Sub
```

When you have extended the program with all the changes mentioned in this section, perform the following tests:

- Start the IconList program.
- Load the group of icons from the VB\ICONS\COMPUTER directory.
- Display the icon overview by clicking on the *Icons* button. See what happens when you move the scroll block in the scroll bar.
- Increase the size of the display window to the maximum and move the scroll block a couple of times.

The screen looks very attractive and interesting but it takes a long time before all the changes take effect. We must solve a few problems:

1   Each time that the Windows_Fill procedure is exe-
     cuted, the icon display in the IconList window (cap-
     tion IconsAvailable) has to be removed from the
     screen. This is not difficult: we only need to assign
     the value False to the *Visible* property of the Image-
     List and IconFileList controls. In this way, a coun-
     ter loop will first make *all* the icons in the list invisi-
     ble. This means that only the icons whose numbers
     correspond to the position of the scroll block need
     to appear at the next display event. All others need
     not be shown. To do this, we shall create a new
     general procedure: Icons_Invisible, by selecting
     New Procedure from the *View* menu (Alt-V, N).

```
Sub Icons_Invisible ()
    For Index = 1 To FNameNr
        ImageList(Index).Visible = False
        IconFileList(Index).Visible = False
    Next Index
End Sub
```

Now extend the VertScroll_Change procedure with
a line activating this clearing procedure:

```
Sub VertScroll_Change ()
    Icons_Invisible
    BValue = VertScroll.Value
    Windows_Fill
End Sub
```

2   If the display window is decreased in size until
     there is not enough room for one single icon, the
     program will jam as soon as the Windows_fill pro-
     cedure is activated within the Form_Resize proce-
     dure. The routines in the program 'presume' that at
     least one icon can always be displayed. In order to
     avoid problems, we shall ensure that the window
     always remains large enough to accommodate
     one icon. If the window is made smaller than the
     default value of 2750 twip in both height and width,
     the value 2750 is fixed as the minimum window
     size. The relevant commands to this effect are in-

cluded in the Resize procedure for the Form object:

```
Sub Form_Resize ()
    If IconList.Height <= 2750 Then
↻        IconList.Height = 2750
    If IconList.Width <= 2750 Then
↻        IconList.Width = 2750
```

This procedure will be extended in the following point. (Note that you do not need to conclude an If block with End If when you place all the information on one line concluded by Enter.)

3   The scroll bar has a fixed position in the display window, regardless of the window size. In other words, it does not adjust along with the window. It would be better if the scroll bar were to be always located at the right-hand side of the window and it responded to adjustments in size. To enable this, the *Top, Left, Height* and *Width* properties of the VertScroll scroll bar should be adjusted according to the size of the display window, thus as the Form_Resize procedure is executed.

We can calculate the *Top* property of the scroll bar by taking the top of the inner form area using the *ScaleTop* property and adding the height of the status line. The distance from the left edge is worked out by subtracting the width of the scroll bar from the width of the inner area. The height of the scroll bar is the difference between the height of the work area and the height of the status line. Add the following lines under the If lines mentioned above.

```
    VertScroll.Top = IconList.ScaleTop +
↻       TopLine.Height
    VertScroll.Left = IconList.ScaleWidth -
↻       VertScroll.Width
    VertScroll.Height = IconList.ScaleHeight
↻       - TopLine.Height
```

After these alterations, the contents of the window should be displayed according to the new values:

```
        Icons_Invisible
        Windows_Fill
End Sub
```

This brings us to the end of our ICONLIST project. The program now works in an acceptable way. A couple of small things could be improved. We shall do that in the next chapter. Do not forget to save the project.

Create a new directory called PICS_TV for working in the next chapter. This is done by switching to the Windows File Manager, selecting the VB_EXMPL directory and then *Create Directory* from the *File* menu. Copy the ICONLIST files to this directory as outlined at the beginning of chapter 2.

Exercises

1   Which properties are required to operate the Vert-Scroll scroll bar? Give the full names of these properties and describe their functions.
    a) _____
    b) _____
    c) _____
    d) _____
    e) _____

2   Outline the difference between the *Enabled* and the *Visible* properties in the following cases:
    a) Which values are used to operate these?
        _____

    b) Which effect do these properties have?
        _____

3   Which properties define the sizes of the work area in a form?
        _____

Answers

1   Which properties are required to operate the Vert-
    Scroll scroll bar? Give the full names of these
    properties and describe their functions.
    a) *VertScroll.Min* - defines the smallest valid value
    b) *VertScroll.Max* - defines the largest valid value
    c) *VertScroll.Value* - this defines the value of the
       position of the scroll block in the scroll bar
    d) *VertScroll.SmallChange* - this defines the modi-
       fications made as a result of one click on one of
       the arrows in the scroll bars
    e) *VertScroll.LargeChange* - this defines the modi-
       fications made as a result of one click on one of
       the areas between the scroll block and an ar-
       row in the scroll bar

2   Outline the difference between the *Enabled* and
    the *Visible* properties in the following cases:
    a) Which values are used to operate these?
       True and False.
    b) Which effect do these properties have?
       Visible makes a control visible or invisible, but
       the control itself remains active. *Enabled*
       makes the control itself active or inactive.

    3   Which properties define the sizes of the work
        area in a form?
        ScaleHeight and *ScaleWidth*.

4 The ICONLIST III project

Up until now our ICONLIST project has only dealt with the display of icons. However, the Image control is able to display three different Windows file formats:

- the *icon format* (ICO), with which we are now familiar and which always consists of 32 by 32 pixels
- the *bitmap format* (BMP), for images which can be freely adjusted in height and width
- the *Windows metafile format* (WMF), which is based not on pixels like the others, but on descriptions of complete graphic objects such as circles lines and areas.

In this chapter, we shall illustrate that the program we have developed for icons is also suitable for other types of images.

4.1 ICONLIST III, the project description

The ICONLIST III project is an extension of ICONLIST II. The new functions are:

- selection and display of the icon (ICO), bitmap (BMP) and Windows metafile (WMF) image formats via the Combo box control,
- a routine to handle errors, operated by the program,
- a facility to copy objects to the Windows Clipboard where possible,
- a command button to open an Info window which shows a time-operated animation,
- operation of the program via the keyboard.

4.2   ICONLIST III, extending the work area

The ICON-TV form

The Info window is opened by means of a command button in the IconTV form. Place a command button in this form under the *Icons* button.

In order to be able to make a selection of one of the three types of file formats, we shall use file name patterns. In a Combo box you can open a list of options which contain all valid values. You can select one of these. Create a Combo box and place it under the display field for the list of files. To round it off neatly, place a label box immediately above the Combo box.

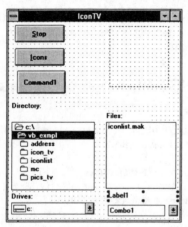

The INFO.FRM form

The Info form (which will be given the name InfoWindow) will ultimately look like this:

Open a new form (Form1) and place three label boxes, a command button, three image controls and a control for a clock. The clock operates the processes whose code is executed in specified intervals. During the program execution this control is not visible.

Save this Form1 file under the name INFO.FRM.

4.3 ICONLIST III, defining the properties

Open the Project window. Double click on the ICON-LIST.FRM. Select *Properties* from the *Window* menu. Open the list of properties and click on IconList Form. Specify the properties as shown.

ICONLIST.FRM form

IconList Form
Caption   = Gallery

Do the same for the ICON_TV form.

ICON_TV.FRM

IconTV Form
Caption   = PicsTV

IconSwitch CommandButton
Caption   = &Pictures

A Combo box possesses the features of an options list which only shows currently valid values, and also the features of a text box which can accept specified input. A Combo box presents a series of valid options but also accepts other values. The *Style* property defines the type of Combo box. Visual Basic provides three types of Combo boxes:

■ **Dropdown Combo** (Style = 0): the list contains a text box for specified input and a drop-down list so that you can select from the standard input.

■ **Simple Combo** (Style = 1): similar to the Dropdown Combo but permanently visible. You can adjust the height of the list when in the design mode.

■ **Dropdown List** (Style = 2): with this type of list Combo box, the list of options is only visible after a click on the arrow. The registrations in the list here cannot be altered.

If the list contains more options than can be shown in one box, the Combo box is automatically given a scroll bar. The list appears automatically at the top if there is not sufficient space under the Combo box.

Style = 0 - Dropdown Combo   Style = 2 - Dropdown List

Style = 1 - Simple Combo

In our project we shall use *Style=2*, because we must choose from a fixed number of options: ICO, BMP, WMF and all files.

Combo1 ComboBox
Height   = 300
Left   = 2700
Name   = Extension
Style   = 2 - Dropdown List
TabIndex   = 3
Top   = 4860
Width   = 1905

Command1 CommandButton
Caption   = In&fo
Height   = 465
Left   = 180
Name   = Info
TabIndex   = 6
Top   = 1440
Width   = 1365

Label1 Label
Caption   = File Type:
Height   = 195
Left   = 2700
Name   = InfoLabel
Top   = 4590
Width   = 1185

Switch to the form being created, INFO.FRM. Open the *Window* menu, select *Project*. Double click on INFO.FRM. Open the *Window* menu. Select *Properties*.

INFO.FRM form

Form1 Form
BorderStyle   = 3 - Fixed Double
Caption   = Info about ...
Height   = 2625
Left   = 2700
Name   = InfoWindow
Top   = 2295
Width   = 3075

Command1 CommandButton
Caption	= &OK
Height	= 465
Left	= 900
Name	= InfoBOK
TabIndex	= 0
Top	= 1620
Width	= 1095

Image1 Image
Height	= 480
Left	= 180
Name	= InfoIcon
Top	= 810
Width	= 480

Image2 Image
Height	= 480
Left	= 2400
Name	= IMouthShut
Top	= 1800
Width	= 480

Image3 Image
Height	= 480
Left	= 2400
Name	= IMouthOpen
Top	= 1320
Width	= 480

The appearance of text on the screen depends on various properties:

Property	Valid values
FontName	depends on the fonts installed
FontSize	depends on the font chosen
FontBold	True/False
FontItalic	True/False
FontStrikethru	True/False
FontUnderline	True/False

Specify the properties of the Label boxes as follows:

Label1 Label
Alignment	= 2 - Center
Caption	= PicsTV
FontName	= Times New Roman (click on the property and open the drop down list. Click on the appropriate font.)
FontSize	= 18
Height	= 465
Left	= 90
Top	= 90
Width	= 2715

Label2 Label
Caption	= Version 1.0
FontItalic	= True
FontName	= Times New Roman
FontSize	= 9.75
Height	= 285
Left	= 990
Top	= 450
Width	= 1005

The copyright character is generated under Windows by pressing Alt-0169 (NumLock on). If you do not know how to produce a certain character, open the Character Map application in the Accessories group and click on the required character. The bottom right-hand corner will indicate which key or key combination is used to generate the character.

Label3 Label
Alignment	= 2 - Center
Caption	= © Spectrum Publishers
FontName	= Times New Roman
FontSize	= 8.25
Height	= 465
Left	= 900
Top	= 840
Width	= 1905

Timer1 Timer
Left   = 240
Top   = 1560

4.4   ICONLIST III, extending the program code

The IconTV form, ICON_TV.FRM

In the first stage we shall define the valid file types for the display of the pictures. These file types must be included in the options list in the Combo box. Because these data must be available when the IconTV form is opened, we shall have to call them up in the Form_Load procedure.

The AddItem method adds a registration to the options list in a Combo box. The *ListIndex* property indicates which registration is being displayed in the options list input field at any given moment. The value 0 represents the first registration. In our example that is *Icon (*.ICO)*.

Click on ICON_TV.FRM in the Project window. Click on View Code. Activate Form in the Object box. Add the program lines shown in boldface below:

```
Sub Form_Load ()
     Extension.AddItem "Icon (*.ICO)"
     Extension.AddItem "Bitmap (*.BMP)"
     Extension.AddItem "Metafile (*.WMF)"
     Extension.AddItem "All files"
     Extension.ListIndex = 0

     Way.Caption = Dir1.Path
     File1.Pattern = "*.ico"
     Dir1_Change
End Sub
```

The options list contains only text at the moment; the program does not yet know which extension belongs to which registration. Therefore, we have to create a link between the selected option in the list and the corresponding extension. This is done via the *ListIndex* property; the extension is allocated to the *Pattern* property of the File1 file options list. The *Pattern* property may also contain different extensions as long as they are separated from one another by a semi-colon and a space.

Select Case

In our program, we have come to the stage that a selection can be made between four alternatives. It is not easy to program the selection of these alternatives using the If-Then-Else construction. It can be done by placing four blocks in a row, but the *Select Case* structure is more direct and clear in this instance.

The top line of the Select Case structure consists of the *Select Case* command with the variable which is to be interpreted. In the block which follows, the further continuation is specified, according to each value. An additional block deals with the case in which an option is chosen for which there is no command block. When the relevant block has been executed, the program continues further after the *End Select* command.

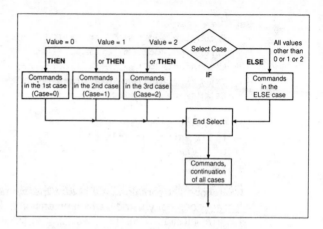

The program uses the selection structure in the Extension_Click procedure to examine whether Extension.ListIndex can be given the index of one of the four registrations in the list. For this to take place, the index must lie between 0 and 3. All other values are ignored, so that we do not have to create a *Case Else* block.

The activation of the Dir1_Change procedure adapts the contents of the file options list to the new value of the *Pattern* variable. In the ICON_TV.FRM code window, click on Extension in the Object list and then on Click in the Proc: list. Type the lines shown in boldface below:

```
Sub Extension_Click ()
    Select Case (Extension.ListIndex)
        Case 0
            File1.Pattern = "*.ico"
        Case 1
            File1.Pattern = "*.bmp"
        Case 2
            File1.Pattern = "*.wmf"
        Case 3
            File1.Pattern = "*.ico; *.bmp; *.wmf"
```

```
        End Select
        Dirl_Change
End Sub
```

Save the input and test the program. You will find a number of files with the BMP format in the \WINDOWS directory. Change the extension in the extension box to .BMP (under the File Type:).

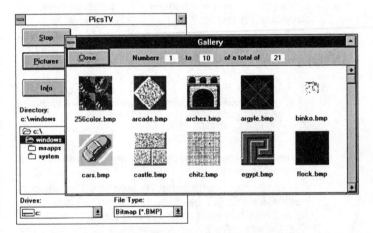

The sizes of the pictures in BMP and WMF files can vary in height and width, while the Image box in the IconTV form is square. The *Stretch* property adjusts the display of the picture to the window which can lead to the result being deformed.

Do not end the program yet; implement the following test which is a precursor of the second step in the extension of the program. Remove any diskettes which may be in the floppy diskdrives. In the Drives list box in the lower left-hand corner, click on the arrow pointing downwards and then on drive A:. This interrupts the program and causes an error message.

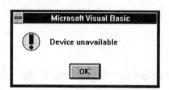

The error message is caused by Visual Basic discovering that the specified drive does not contain a diskette (this type of message can also be caused by the directory being unreadable). The program is now discontinued and we cannot do anything about it at the moment. Activating the PicsTV window does not restart the program.

Acknowledge the error message by clicking on *OK* and quit the program by selecting *End* from the *Run* menu (Alt-R, E).

Dealing with error messages in the program

Up until now, we have not applied any measures to rectify any (operating) errors which cause Visual Basic to react with an error message and a discontinuation of the program. We intend to anticipate errors (so-called *trappable errors*) in the execution of the program and to deal with them before Visual Basic reacts to them by stopping the program execution.

The *On Error GoTo* construction is only executed when an error occurs. The location of the program block containing the error-handling routine is placed behind the *GoTo* section. If no error occurs, the program control will quit the procedure via the *Exit Sub* command.

```
Sub Drive1_Change ()
    On Error GoTo Drive1_Change_ErrorMessage
    Dir1.Path = Drive1.Drive
Exit Sub
```

The *Exit Sub* command bounds the section which is normally executed. Then follows the label which ends with a colon. This is the reference point of the error-handling routine. The following line is thus the start of this routine:

```
Drivel_Change_ErrorMessage:
```

If an error occurs, Visual Basic generates values for the *Err* (error number) and *Erl* (error line) variables. We shall only use the error number because we can deduce the nature of the error from this. The *Error$* contains a string with an error message which is generated by Visual Basic itself.

The Visual Basic help function provides a list of all *Trappable Errors*. Select *Contents* from the *Help* menu (Alt-H, C) and click on *Trappable Errors*. This opens a window containing a list of all trappable errors. You can obtain information about any specific error by clicking on the green, underlined error name. The error which we forced above, Device Unavailable, is registered under number 68.

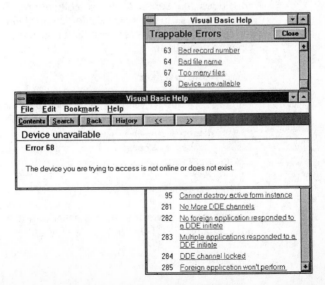

We use the Select Case construction to request the error number of the *Err* variable. If *Err=68*, Visual Basic displays the rather vague message that the device is unavailable. This is generally an indication that the drive does not contain a diskette or that the diskette is not formatted. We shall alter this standard message so that the program shows a capital letter to represent the diskdrive. We shall place the combined message in the *Msg* variable, which is displayed in a message box. In the case of error numbers 70 and 71, we shall take the easy way out by assigning, in the *Error$* variable, the standard Visual Basic error text to the *Msg* variable.

Just as in the case of the For-Next loop construction, there is also an initial value and an ending value respectively in front of, and behind, the *To* command in the Select Case construction. Because we are dealing with only two values here, we can also type *Case 70, 71*. All other trappable errors are dealt with in the block behind *Case Else*. This block compiles the error messages out of the error number followed by a colon and the standard error text. The Str$() function converts a numerical value to a string. The *End Select* command concludes the series of predictable errors. The program listing is thus as follows after Drive1_Change_ErrorMessage: label (after Exit Sub) in the Drive1_-Change subroutine:

```
    Select Case Err
        Case 68
            Msg = " Drive " + UCase$(Drivel.Drive)
                    + " unavailable. "
        Case 70 To 71
            Msg = Error$
    Case Else
        Msg = Str$(Err) + " : " + Error$
    End Select
```

The program shows the error message in a message box containing a STOP sign and an OK button.

```
    MsgBox Msg, 16
```

We must make sure that the incorrectly specified drive does not remain the currently active drive. The previous drive is again activated. Its value is still available in the *Dir1.Path* variable.

```
Drive1.Drive = Dir1.Path
```

The error handling routine ends with the *Resume* command. The addition *Next* means that once the error handling routine has been executed, the program proceeds to the command which follows the "jump" command in the listing. In our example, that is the *Exit Sub* line.

```
    Resume Next
End Sub
```

For the sake of clarity, we show the entire error-handling procedure here:

```
Sub Drive1_Change ()
    On Error GoTo Drive1_Change_ErrorMessage
    Dir1.Path = Drive1.Drive
Exit Sub
Drive1_Change_ErrorMessage:
    Select Case Err
        Case 68
            Msg = " Drive " + UCASE$(Drive1.Drive)
                + " unavailable. "
        Case 70 To 71
            Msg = Error$
    Case Else
        Msg = Str$(Err) + " : " + Error$
    End Select
    MsgBox Msg, 16
    Drive1.Drive = Dir1.Path
    Resume Next
End Sub
```

Copying images to the Clipboard

It is possible to exchange data and images between different applications when working under Windows. In our program, we shall copy the contents of the Image box called Imidge to the Clipboard by means of a double click.

Unfortunately, it is not possible to copy icons to the Clipboard. Therefore we shall ensure that our program shows a message to this effect when the user attempts to copy in this way. The program will check, after the double click, whether or not the chosen file contains an icon by comparing the last three letters of the chosen filename with those of an icon file (ICO). If this condition is met, the program creates the relevant error message box.

The command CHR$(13) generates the ANSI character Carriage Return. This value is identical to the code which is produced by pressing the Enter key. The effect of this is that the message continues on the next line. This occurs automatically when a text is too long to be displayed on one line in the message box.

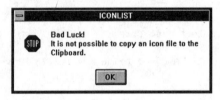

```
Sub Imidge_DblClick ()
    If Right$(File1.FileName, 3) = "ico" Then
        Msg = "Bad Luck!" + CHR$(13) + "It is
↻           not possible to copy an icon file
↻           to the Clipboard."
        MsgBox Msg, 16
    Else
        ClipBoard.Clear
```

```
        ClipBoard.SetData Imidge.Picture
        M$ = "The file    " +
⇨          UCASE$(File1.FileName) +"   has
⇨          been copied to the Clipboard."
        MsgBox M$, 48
    End If
End Sub
```

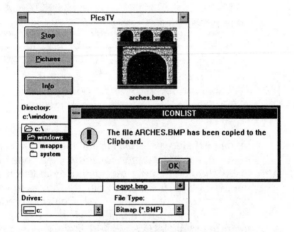

You can import the copied image file from the Clipboard into another application such as Paintbrush for instance.

The figure on the next page shows that the ARCHES.BMP image has been altered to form a square due to the *Stretch=True* property of the Imidge Image box.

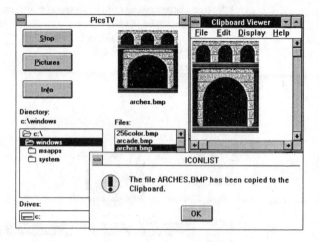

In the next step, we shall include the Clipboard function in the IconList form; the procedure itself does not need to be structurally adjusted to accommodate this. Only the selection of the image from the list has to be coded differently: instead of the *File1.FileName* property we shall use the current element *Fylename (Index-1)* from the array variable *Fylename ()* which we declared as a global variable. Just as previously, we shall have to deal with the difference in numbers between the index for the filenames and the controls.

In the ICON_TV.FRM form, go to the Imidge_DblClick procedure and mark the code section from *If* to *End If* and copy this section to the Clipboard using the *Copy* command from the *Edit* menu (Alt-E, C or Ctrl-C). Switch to the ICONLIST.FRM form and go to the code of the new DblClick procedure for the ImageList() object. Paste the contents of the Clipboard (using *Edit, Paste* or Alt-E, P or Ctrl-V) into the procedure. Then change the text as shown in boldface below:

```
Sub ImageList_DblClick (Index As Integer)
    If Right$(Fylename(Index - 1), 3) =
⇨        "ico" Then
```

```
        Msg = "Bad Luck!" + CHR$(13) + "It is
↻          not possible to copy an icon file
↻          to the Clipboard."
        MsgBox Msg, 16
    Else
        ClipBoard.Clear
        ClipBoard.SetData ImageList(Index).Picture
        M$ = "The file    " +
↻          UCASE$(Fylename(Index - 1)) +
↻          "    has been copied to the Clipboard."
        MsgBox M$, 48
    End If
End Sub
```

A simple animation

We shall program a simple animation film in the Info-Window (INFO.FRM). This animation is operated by means of the clock (the TIMER control). The window is closed by means of the *OK* command button.

The InfoWindow is displayed from within the IconTV form by means of the *Info* button. The *Show* method is used for this, which we also used when displaying the IconList window.

```
Sub Info_Click ()
    InfoWindow.Show 1
End Sub
```

The InfoWindow form, INFO.FRM

We shall use the three Smily icons for the animation, FACE01.ICO, FACE02.ICO and FACE03.ICO. These files are stored in the \VB\ICONS\MISC directory. Start the current version of the project and examine the icons mentioned in the IconList window. The animation will begin with FACE01.ICO and then FACE02.ICO and FACE03.ICO will replace one another with a speed which we shall specify in the program.

We shall make the icon display a fixed component of the InfoWindow form. This guarantees that if you copy this project for someone else, the icons used in the program are accessible for the other person (as long as the directory path in the other computer is identical). Taking the InfoIcon control as the starting point, we shall make the link via the *Picture* property. A double click on the *Picture* property in the Properties window opens the *Load Picture* dialog window.

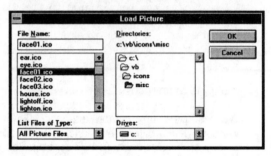

Activate the FACE01.ICO file in the \VB\ICONS\MISC directory. As soon as you click on *OK*, the icon appears in the InfoIcon Image field. Link the FACE02.ICO and FACE03.ICO files to the IMouthShut and IMouthOpen Image fields respectively, in the same way. A link to an icon file can be recognized in the properties list of the controls by the value (Icon) of *Picture*.

We wish to have the FACE02 and FACE03 icons appear in the InfoIcon Image box when the InfoWindow form is shown. Although they are to be shown in the InfoWindow, they are to be invisible when the program is being run. Accordingly, assign the value False to the *Visible* property of both IMouthOpen and IMouthShut.

To operate the continual switching of the icons in the InfoIcon Image box, we shall use the Timer1 control. We specify the speed of change by means of the *Interval* property. This value defines the time in milliseconds between the two activations of the icons. Thus, the value 500 is equal to an interval of half a second. Assign the value 500 to the *Timer1.Interval* property.

In order to prevent the Timer being obstructed by other procedures, the *MouthOpen* operating variable should be declared with the definition *Static*. This results in the value being available during the entire program. Otherwise the variable will be created at the beginning of the procedure and cleared when the procedure is ended.

The switching back and forth between IMouthOpen and IMouthShut is operated by the *MouthOpen* variable. In this, we shall make use of the settings True and False in a variable of the Integer type. We reserve a branch in the If-Then-Else structure for each of the two icons. If *MouthOpen=True*, the mouth will be open and if *MouthOpen=False*, the mouth will be shut. Then we are faced with the problem of how to code the commands which are to implement the switching back-and-forth between the two Smilies. The *Not* operator converts the logical value of MouthOpen to its opposite at the end of the command block each time: True then becomes False and False becomes True.

```
Sub Timer1_Timer ()
    Static MouthOpen As Integer
    If MouthOpen Then
        InfoIcon.Picture = IMouthOpen.Picture
    Else
        InfoIcon.Picture = IMouthShut.Picture
    End If
    MouthOpen = Not MouthOpen
End Sub
```

The *OK* command button (InfoBOK) closes the Info-Window (the INFO.FRM form). We use the *Unload* command for this control.

```
Sub InfoBOK_Click ()
    Unload InfoWindow
End Sub
```

The gallery of icons can be operated from the keyboard

Although Windows and Visual Basic are generally operated by means of the mouse, many controls provide the
possibility of giving commands by means of the keyboard. Accordingly, command buttons often have a
shortcut key (combination). However, a directory list
cannot be operated from the keyboard without additional
specification. It is possible to move the selection bar
through the options in the directory list using the cursor
keys, but the Enter key has no effect. However, Visual
Basic is able to interpret this input by means of the Key-
Press event procedure. Open the code window for the
Dir1_KeyPress procedure in the ICON_TV.FRM form.

Note: The new procedure automatically contains the
specification (KeyAscii As Integer), assuming
that *KeyAscii* is the name of a variable. Since
the ANSI table is valid under Windows and not
ASCII, we shall alter this name to KeyAnsi just
to be clear (although a variable name has only a
symbolic value internally).

The *KeyAnsi* variable contains the numerical value of
the key pressed, according to the ANSI table. In the
case of Enter, that is the value 13. The procedure has
to check whether or not the key being pressed generates the value 13. If so, the directory currently marked
is assigned to Dir1.Path. This value is obtained from
the directory list (Dir1.List) by means of the index which
is stored in the *ListIndex* property. (Dir1.List contains
all directory registrations and the *ListIndex* property
contains the index of the currently marked option.) Finally, File1.Path has to be brought up to date.

```
Sub Dir1_KeyPress (KeyAnsi As Integer)
    If KeyAnsi = 13 Then
        Dir1.Path = Dir1.List(Dir1.ListIndex)
        File1.Path = Dir1.Path
    End If
End Sub
```

4.5 Creating an EXE file

The program code for the Pics_TV project is now complete. In order to be able to start up the program from Windows, in other words without activating Visual Basic, the program has to be compiled to an executable file whose filename is recognizable by the EXE extension.

Allocating an icon to the program

When you reduce a form to an icon, the standard icon appears with underneath it the text which is shown in the title bar of the form (the value of the *Caption* property). By applying the *Icon* property, you can assign a different icon to the form.

Open the IconTV form and double click on the *Icon* property in the Properties window. This opens the Load Icon dialog window. We shall make it easy on ourselves and choose an icon we already know: FACE03.ICO from the \VB\ICONS\MISC directory.

Note: If you want to design your own icon, the \VB\SAMPLES\ICONWRKS directory contains a Visual Basic project called IconWorks.

Now give the command *Make EXE File* from the *File* menu (Alt-F, K).

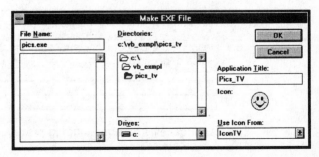

Type the program title, *Pics_TV*, in the Application Title: text box. If necessary, specify the icon from the
IconTV form in the Use Icon From: box. The File Name:
box already contains the name *iconlist.exe* which is de-
rived from the name of the project. Change this to
pics.exe and click on *OK* to start the compiler.

Now you can adopt your first application into one of the
program groups of the Program Manager.

Note: If you pass an executable application which has
been written in Visual Basic on to someone
else, keep in mind that the EXE file is not complete without other files and modules. You can
find out exactly which files belong to the package, over and above the EXE file and the
VBRUN300.DLL file, by reading chapter 25
(*Distributing Your Applications*) of the Visual Basic *Programmer's Guide*.

Exercises

1   Which property enables you to define the type of
Combo box and which types are available?
_____
_____

2   Which properties influence the appearance of
text?
_____
_____

3   Describe the Select Case structure and the possibilities of application.
_____
_____
_____

4   What benefits do error-handling procedures bring
to a program?
_____

5   Which result is obtained by declaring a variable as being *Static*?

6   For which purposes can the Timer control be used and how is it operated?

Answers

1   Which property enables you to define the type of Combo box and which types are available?

The *Style* property. The types are: 0 - Dropdown Combo, 1 - Simple Combo, 2 - Dropdown List.

2   Which properties influence the appearance of text?

FontName, FontSize, FontBold, FontItalic, Font-Strikethru, FontUnderline.

3   Describe the Select Case structure and the possibilities of application.

Structure: *Select Case* operating variable; *Case 1; ...; Case n; Else Case; End Select.*

If more than two possible values of a variable have to be interpreted, the Select Case structure provides the advantage of being quicker and easier to program than nesting structures of the If-Then-Else type.

4   What benefits do error-handling procedures bring to a program?

A program is much more convenient in use when it reacts to predictable operating errors (trappable errors) with an error message than when it suddenly discontinues due to an erroneous action.

5   Which result is obtained by declaring a variable as being *Static*?

Defining a variable as being *Static* results in the variable being available during the entire run-through of the program. A normal local variable is only available in the procedure in which it was declared.

6   For which purposes can the Timer control be used and how is it operated?

The Timer control can regulate processes in which it is necessary to execute program blocks at certain intervals. The *Interval* property defines the speed of operation in milliseconds.

5   The Music Catalogue project, MC

In this chapter we shall create a program for data management. Data management is only practical if there is a file containing amounts of the same type of data, gathered together into specific groups. The various data which form one group are stored in *fields*. A group of fields together is called a *record*. Data management is only possible if all records in the file have the same structure, in other words, if all records consist of the same fields and these fields have the same order of sequence, the same length and are of the same type. The collection of all records is called a *datafile*. Our example program in this chapter is to manage data about sound devices in a fictional sound library (LPs, CDs, tapes etc.). You can make a similar program for any other chosen collection: addresses, books, postage stamps, comic books, butterflies etc.

General file management

Data can be managed in various ways:

■ **Sequential**
   All records are stored consecutively without any further structuring being applied. Any specific record can only be found by looking through the entire list from the first record onwards. The selection procedure is performed by means of a given attribute, a *key*.

■ **Index sequential**
   In order to be able to find a specific record in a file as quickly as possible, each record has its own index, its own record number. In this system, all records must have an identical structure: the corresponding fields are of the same type and their length is identical. For any given number, the pro-

gram calculates the location of the record from the product of the number and the length of the individual records.

■ **Multiple files (database)**
   In the management of a database (a collection of datafiles which have some kind of mutual relationship), the datafiles are stored in the form of separate tables or lists. A row in the table corresponds to one record. Each column in the table contains the various data from one field. It is possible to link different tables to one another by means of cross-reference. This provides the advantage that one piece of information, such as the name of a customer for instance, only needs to occur once in the entire database. By means of reference to other files, all information in the database which is relevant to this customer (e.g. orders or turnover) can be made accessible.

The following sections are constructed in such a way that you can become familiar with all aspects of data management by means of a simple programming example. A file in memory is our point of departure and we shall execute various procedures according to the index sequential method. The file can only be stored on disk in a sequential fashion. In our example project we shall not use any linked files (database) since Visual Basic in its straightforward form does not support this method.

5.1   The Music Catalogue, project description

The Music Catalogue program is meant to register data about a music collection. For this we shall create a kind of filing cabinet with a card for each registration. Each card is to display the following information:

- Artist: the name of the artist or group
- Title: the name of the CD or LP etc.
- Type: the type of sound device: CD, LP, cassette recorder or DAT
- Number: the numerical value representing the number of devices (e.g. 2 for a double CD)
- Genre: the kind of music
- Notes: various pieces of general information not fitting the categories above.

The work area

There is an input mask which enables you to add, alter or remove a record. The mask contains input boxes for all fields in the record. It also enables you to browse through the records in the file. Thus, the mask represents a kind of card index or filing cabinet.

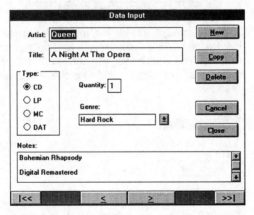

The program can reproduce a display of the data on the screen or printer, and via a screen line you can open the mask of the corresponding record. There is a menu available to alter the design of the lists which are displayed. A status line at the bottom of the window displays information concerning the currently active file and the number of records it contains. The window in the figure below shows the standard display.

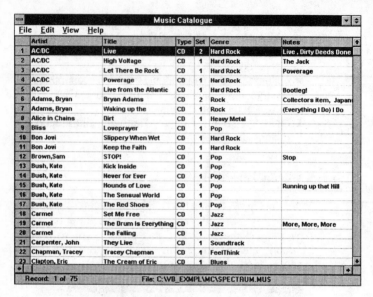

The *File* menu contains commands for creating a new file, for opening an existing file and for saving the current file. The *Print* command conveys the current file to the printer. The last command in the list closes the program.

The edit mask can be opened in two ways: either by double clicking on a registration in the list or by opening the *Edit* menu.

You can activate or deactivate the status line via the *View* menu. In addition, you can use this menu to open the *Selection* dialog box (mask). This enables you to specify which data fields should be included in the lists. The *View* menu also contains the *Font* option which enables you to specify a chosen font, and also the *Point Size* option for the size of the font. The *Background Colour* option enables you to give the background a different colour.

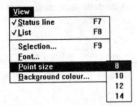 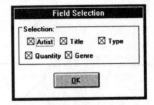

The *Info* command from the *Help* menu opens an information window which provides information about our Music Catalogue program.

We shall make use of the standard dialog windows provided by the Common Dialog control for the options we wish to apply: *Open, Save* and *Print* from the *File* menu and also for the *Font* and *Background Colour* options from the *View* menu.

Data management

The actual management of the currently active file takes place in working memory (RAM). The program addresses the chosen record by means of its index. This record is copied to a temporary record in the record buffer. All input in the edit mask is first stored in the record buffer. Confirmed alterations for each record are then copied back to the file. The datafile is thus always up to date (except for alterations to the current record which have not yet been confirmed). The datafile is loaded from and written to disk.

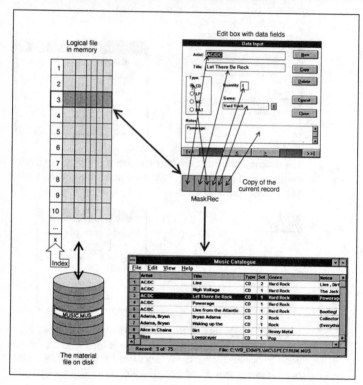

5.2   The MusicMain form, MAIN.FRM

Creating the work area

We create the first form of the new project by means of the *New Project* command from the *File* menu (Alt-F, N). The entire project is to be menu-driven. The Form1 form is the basic window from where the other windows can be opened when required.

The *Menu Design* option from the *Window* menu (Alt-W, M or Ctrl-M) opens a dialog window in which all actions for the construction of the menus in the current form are carried out.

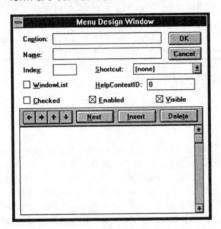

Just like a control, each menu item has its own properties. We are already acquainted with the *Caption, Name* and *Index* properties from preceding chapters. The *Index* property is used later to operate the program by means of "jump" commands to procedures. A menu item at the highest level (the menu name which is always visible in the menu bar) has no *Index*.

We shall begin with the first menu, which is given the title *File*. Type *&File* in the Caption text box. Press the Tab key to go to Name text box and type the internal name for the menu, *FileMenu*. Click on the *Next* command button to move on to the next menu item.

The first command in the *File* drop-down menu is to be *New*. Type *&New* in the Caption text box and *MFile* in the Name text box. At this moment, File and New are at the same level in the hierarchy; but *New* is to be the first menu item in the *File* menu. This is done by moving the item at the lower level a little to the right just as in a table of contents. The dialog window contains command buttons with arrows. The buttons with arrows pointing left and right change the indentation of the current menu item.

Click on the arrow pointing right. The *New* menu item shifts to the right. The lower level is indicated by four dots.

Carry out these steps for the following menu items. Begin each time with *Next*.

The OPEN command

Caption	= &Open
Name	= MFile
Index	= 1

The *Shortcut* property enables you to give a command from the keyboard, outside the menu structure. In that case, it is not necessary to open the relevant menu. We shall define the Shortcut key combination Ctrl-S for the *Save* menu item. This key combination is assigned to the menu item by means of the *Shortcut* options list in the dialog window.

The *Enabled* check box indicates whether the current menu item is active (a cross means True) or inactive (no cross means False). Our intention is to have *Save* available only when there is a file in memory, thus after a *New* or *Open* command. Accordingly, the standard setting for this option will be inactive. When the program is run, the status of this point can change as a result of the two commands mentioned. The *Visible* check box regulates whether or not the menu item is visible.

The SAVE command

Caption	= &Save
Name	= MFile
Index	= 2
Shortcut	= Ctrl+S
Enabled	= False

Three dots behind a menu item indicate that the command will open a dialog window.

The SAVE AS... command

Caption	= Save &As...
Name	= MFile
Index	= 3
Enabled	= False

A menu becomes more clear by dividing the menu items according to function. To bring this about, we shall add a menu item whose title consists of only one dash (hyphen). Do not forget that the dividing line must also have an index. A menu item like this is managed by Visual Basic just like any other menu item.

LINE

Caption	= -
Name	= MFile
Index	= 4

The PRINT... command

Caption	= &Print...
Name	= MFile
Index	= 5
Shortcut	= Ctrl+P
Enabled	= False

Create a dividing line to separate the last command.

LINE

Caption	= -
Name	= MFile
Index	= 6

The EXIT command

Caption	= E&xit
Name	= MFile
Index	= 7

This completes the *File* menu.

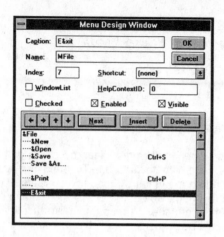

The next registration in the Menu Design is the *Edit* menu. We shall create this menu on the next line of the Menu Design Window. Click on *Next* and remove the indentation by clicking on the arrow pointing left. Then enter the data for the *Edit* menu. This menu does not contain menu items. A click on the menu title works immediately as a command.

The EDIT menu
Caption   = &Edit
Name   = EditMenu

The *View* menu contains, among other things, commands to make the data list and the status line visible or invisible. When these elements are visible, a tick mark is shown in front of the menu item. This part of the menu registration is controlled by the *Checked* check box: a cross means True, no cross means False.

The VIEW menu
Caption   = &View
Name   = ViewMenu

The STATUS LINE command

Caption	= &Status line
Name	= MView
Index	= 0
Shortcut	= F7
Checked	= True

The LIST command

Caption	= &List
Name	= MView
Index	= 1
Shortcut	= F8

LINE

Caption	= -
Name	= MView
Index	= 2

The SELECTION... command

Caption	= Se&lection...
Name	= MView
Index	= 3
Shortcut	= F9

The FONT... command

Caption	= &Font...
Name	= MView
Index	= 4

The POINT SIZE...command

Caption	= &Point size
Name	= MView
Index	= 5

The *Point size* menu option automatically opens a sub-menu with the available point sizes for the current font. This submenu is located at a lower level and therefore in the Menu Design window it is placed further to the right.

The 8 command
Caption   = 8
Name   = MLetter
Index   = 0

The 10 command
Caption   = 10
Name   = MLetter
Index   = 1

The 12 command
Caption   = 12
Name   = MLetter
Index   = 2

The 14 command
Caption   = 14
Name   = MLetter
Index   = 3

This concludes the structure of the submenu. Click on the arrow pointing leftwards to return to one level higher in the menu hierarchy.

The BACKGROUND COLOUR LIST... command
Caption   = &Background colour...
Name   = MView
Index   = 6

The HELP menu
Caption   = &Help
Name   = InfoMenu

The INFO... command

Caption	= &Info...
Name	= MInfo
Index	= 0

This concludes the input for the design of the menu structure. Close the Menu Design window by clicking on *OK*. If Visual Basic encounters something which is incorrect, because you have forgotten something or that you have assigned the same index in one menu for instance, an error message will be shown.

Save the result under the name MAIN.FRM in the \VB_EXMPL\MC directory by selecting *Save File As...* from the *File* menu (Alt-F, A or Ctrl-A). Do that also with the *Save Project As...* command from the *File* menu (Alt-F, E). Specify the name MC.MAK.

Start the program and check if the menus are correct. Because the *Edit* menu is also a command, it does not open like the other menus: the registration is only visible as long as you hold down the mouse button. If you operate the menus by means of the keyboard, the registration remains visible: in that case, a command has to be confirmed by pressing Enter.

 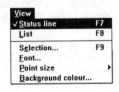

Notes: You can also check the menus in the form, but this method has the disadvantage that clicking on a menu item will open the code window for the corresponding procedure. You can avoid this by using the cursor keys instead of the mouse.

The standard dialog windows, Common dialog

The Common dialog control makes the routines of the
Dynamic Link Library COMMDLG.DLL under Windows
available for Visual Basic. This library is only accessible if the COMMDLG.DLL and CMDIALOG.VBX files
are located in the Windows system directory. We shall
make use of the Common dialog control (CMDIA-
LOG.VBX) to make windows for opening, saving and
printing files. We shall also use the dialog windows for
colour and font for the design of file lists.

In the Design mode, the control icon will be visible in
the form. While the project is being executed, the functions which activate the dialog windows will be available but the control itself is not visible and also cannot
be activated.

Normally, the CMDIALOG.VBX control is automatically
included in the project at the start of Visual Basic by
means of the AUTOLOAD.MAK file. Open the project
window and check if the CMDIALOG.VBX control is included in the list. We shall also use the GRID.VBX control in our Music Catalogue project. If one of these controls is absent from this project list, you can add a file to
the project using the *Add File* command from the *File*
menu (Alt-F, D or Ctrl-D).

Place a Common dialog box in the lower right-hand
corner of the Form1 (MAIN.FRM) form.

The Grid control

The Grid control functions as a table consisting of rows
and columns. The position of a cell is determined by
specifying the intersection of the row and the column. A
cell may contain a text or an image. The grid works in
roughly the same way as a worksheet in a spreadsheet
program. The difference is that alterations in the contents of the grid can only take place by means of the
commands which we have included in the program.

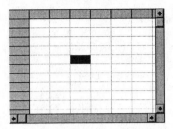

We shall use the grid to display the contents of a data file in list form. Each row in the table will be filled with a record; a column contains the data of one field from different records.

Place a Grid control in Form1.

The status line

The status line also serves as the basis for two label boxes in this example. Create a Picture box and place two Label boxes within it. Keep in mind that you will have to use the 'drag open' method to do this; a double click on the label boxes will place these boxes in the form itself.

Defining the properties

Assign the following properties to Form1 and the controls.

Form1 Form
Caption	= Music Catalogue
Height	= 5000
Icon	= C:\VB\ICONS\MISC\MISC31.ICO
Left	= 615
Name	= MusicMain
Top	= 1140
Width	= 8565

Picture1 PictureBox
Alignment	= 2 - Align Bottom
BackColor	= &H00C0C0C0&
Height	= 300
Name	= StatusLine

Label1 Label
BackColor	= &H00C0C0C0& (light grey)
Caption	= Record:
Height	= 192
Left	= 276
Name	= StatusRec
Top	= 20
Width	= 4500

Label2 Label
BackColor	= &H00C0C0C0& (light grey)
Caption	= File:
Height	= 192
Left	= 3500
Name	= StatusFile
Top	= 20
Width	= 4500

Grid1 Grid
FontName	= Arial
Height	= 1000
Left	= 0
Name	= Overview
Top	= 0
Visible	= False
Width	= 1500

CMDialog1 CommonDialog
Left	= 8000
Top	= 3500

5.3 The MASK.FRM form

The Mask window is to show the contents of the fields in the currently active record and also manages this record. The input boxes enable you to insert or alter the contents of the various fields. There are command buttons to create, copy or delete a record. In addition, there are buttons which enable you to browse through the data file: you can move forwards through a record (>) or backwards (<) or jump to the beginning (|<<) or to the end (>>|) of the file. The *Cancel* button enables you to close the window without saving the modifications. If the modifications are to be saved in the data file, close the window by means of the *Close* button. The design of the form looks like this:

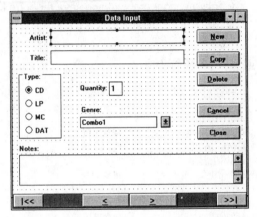

Making the work area

Create a new form by means of the *New Form* command from the *File* menu (Alt-F, F). Place the following controls in this form:

- six Label boxes
- nine Command buttons
- four Text boxes
- one Combo box
- a Frame with four Option buttons.

The Frame control enables you to combine a number
of controls to form one group. Creating this is similar to
the status line. First drag the frame open and then
place the four option buttons within the frame, so that
they form a logical unit as an options list. A single option button can be either on or off. In a group of option
buttons, only one option button may be activated at any
one time: activating one of these buttons deactivates
all the others.

Compile the second form in the MC project using the
controls mentioned above and save the form under the
name MASK.FRM.

Defining the properties

Assign the following properties to the mask form:

Form2 Form
BorderStyle	= 1 - Fixed Single
Caption	= Data Input
ControlBox	= False
Height	= 5340
Left	= 1410
MaxButton	= False
MinButton	= False
Name	= Mask
Top	= 800
Width	= 6600

The *Control Box* property indicates whether or not the
window will have a button for a *Control menu*. Defining
this property as False ensures that the window can
only be closed by means of one of our command buttons.

Label1 Label
BackColor	= &H00808080& (dark grey)
BorderStyle	= 1 - Fixed Single
Caption	=
Height	= 372
Left	= 0

Top	= 4560
Width	= 6492

Command1 CommandButton

Caption	= |<<
FontSize	= 12
Height	= 372
Left	= 0
Name	= MaskBRBegin
TabIndex	= 14
Top	= 4560
Width	= 852

Command2 CommandButton

Caption	= &<
FontSize	= 12
Height	= 372
Left	= 1920
Name	= MaskBRPrevious
TabIndex	= 15
Top	= 4560
Width	= 1332

Command3 CommandButton

Caption	= &>
FontSize	= 12
Height	= 372
Left	= 3240
Name	= MaskBRNext
TabIndex	= 16
Top	= 4560
Width	= 1332

Command4 CommandButton

Caption	= >>|
FontSize	= 12
Height	= 372
Left	= 5640
Name	= MaskBREnd
TabIndex	= 17
Top	= 4560
Width	= 852

Command5 CommandButton
Caption   = &New
Height   = 375
Left   = 5130
Name   = MaskBNew
TabIndex   = 9
Top   = 180
Width   = 1185

Command6 CommandButton
Caption   = &Copy
Height   = 375
Left   = 5130
Name   = MaskBCopy
TabIndex   = 10
Top   = 780
Width   = 1185

Command7 CommandButton
Caption   = &Delete
Height   = 375
Left   = 5130
Name   = MaskBDelete
TabIndex   = 11
Top   = 1320
Width   = 1185

The *Cancel* property specifies that a command button
is the *Cancel* button in the form. This makes it possible
to exit the window without saving the alterations by
pressing the Esc key.

Command8 CommandButton
Cancel   = True
Caption   = C&ancel
Height   = 375
Left   = 5130
Name   = MaskBCancel
TabIndex   = 12
Top   = 2160
Width   = 1185

Command9 CommandButton
Caption   = C&lose
Height   = 375
Left   = 5130
Name   = MaskBClose
TabIndex   = 13
Top   = 2760
Width   = 1185

Label2 Label
Alignment   = 1 - Right Justify
Caption   = Artist:
Height   = 195
Left   = 70
Top   = 270
Width   = 925

The *MaxLength* property defines the maximum number of characters that can be imported from a text box. If there are more characters than *MaxLength* specifies, the extra characters are excluded and ignored. Delete the value of the *Text* property so that the field is empty when it is displayed for the first time.

Text1 TextBox
FontSize   = 9.75
Height   = 375
Left   = 1080
MaxLength   = 30
Name   = MaskArtist
TabIndex   = 0
Text   =
Top   = 180
Width   = 3705

Label3 Label
Alignment   = i - Right Justify
Caption   = Title:
Height   = 195
Left   = 120
Top   = 810
Width   = 825

Text2 TextBox
FontSize   = 9.75
Height   = 375
Left   = 1080
MaxLength   = 30
Name   = MaskTitle
TabIndex   = 1
Text   =
Top   = 720
Width   = 3705

Label4 Label
Caption   = Quantity:
Height   = 195
Left   = 1890
Top   = 1620
Width   = 760

Text3 TextBox
FontSize   = 9.75
Height   = 375
Left   = 2700
MaxLength   = 2
Name   = MaskQuantity
TabIndex   = 6
Text   = 1
Top   = 1560
Width   = 375

Label5 Label
Caption   = Genre:
Height   = 195
Left   = 1890
Top   = 2200
Width   = 1000

In a Combo box, the elements in the list are sorted automatically if the *Sorted* property has the value *True*.

Combo1 ComboBox
Left   = 1890
Name   = MaskGenre
Sorted   = True

TabIndex	= 7
Top	= 2500
Width	= 2500

Label6 Label

Caption	= Notes:
Height	= 195
Left	= 180
Top	= 3240
Width	= 1275

The *MultiLine* property makes it possible to display a lengthy text by dividing the text into several lines according to the specified text width. With very lengthy texts which do not fit into the text window, it is possible to place horizontal and vertical scroll bars. The value of the *ScrollBars* property defines the number of scroll bars:

ScrollBars

0   none
1   horizontal
2   vertical
3   horizontal and vertical

Text4 TextBox

Height	= 825
Left	= 180
MaxLength	= 200
MultiLine	= True
Name	= MaskNotes
ScrollBars	= 2 - Vertical
TabIndex	= 8
Text	=
Top	= 3510
Width	= 6195

Frame1 Frame

Caption	= Type:
Height	= 1815
Left	= 180
Top	= 1260
Width	= 1185

The four option buttons form a logical unit. The current index of the buttons will indicate which button is currently active at any given moment. Accordingly, we shall give the *Index* property of the buttons a value beginning at 0. By assigning the value True to the *Value* property of one of the option buttons, we ensure that one of the option buttons is activated each time a new mask is opened.

Option1 OptionButton
Caption	= CD
Height	= 285
Index	= 0
Left	= 180
Name	= MaskOption
TabIndex	= 2
Top	= 360
Value	= True
Width	= 735

Option2 OptionButton
Caption	= LP
Height	= 285
Index	= 1
Left	= 180
Name	= MaskOption
TabIndex	= 3
Top	= 720
Width	= 735

Option3 OptionButton
Caption	= MC (music cassette)
Height	= 285
Index	= 2
Left	= 180
Name	= MaskOption
TabIndex	= 4
Top	= 1080
Width	= 735

Option4 OptionButton
Caption   = DAT
Height   = 285
Index   = 3
Left   = 180
Name   = MaskOption
TabIndex   = 4
Top   = 1440
Width   = 735

The input mask is now complete. Save the form (MASK.FRM) and save the project also.

5.4   The SelectionList form, SELEC-TION.FRM

By means of the SelectionList window we can specify which fields from the data file are to be shown in the list. The choice of the available fields is entirely free.

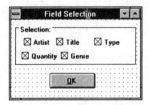

Creating the work area

The selection of the data fields to be displayed is made by means of the Check box control. In contrast to option buttons, check boxes work completely independently: they can be activated and deactivated independent of any other check box settings. However, it remains possible to define relationships between check boxes if required, such as forbidden or necessary combinations for instance.

The SelectionList form is to contain two command buttons, one frame and five check boxes. The five check boxes are to be placed within the frame and therefore have to be opened using the 'drag open' method. They have thus a lower place in the hierarchy.

Save the new form under the name SELECT.FRM.

Defining the properties

Give this mask form the following properties:

Form3 Form
BorderStyle	= 3 - Fixed Double
Caption	= Field Selection
ControlBox	= False
Height	= 2500
Left	= 2500
Name	= SelectionList
Top	= 1200
Width	= 3700

Frame1 Frame
Caption	= Selection:
Height	= 1100
Left	= 120
Top	= 120
Width	= 3350

Check1 CheckBox
Caption	= Artist
Height	= 290
Index	= 0
Left	= 180
Name	= Selection
TabIndex	= 1
Top	= 335
Value	= 1 - Checked
Width	= 835

Check2 CheckBox
Caption	= Title
Height	= 290
Index	= 1
Left	= 1140
Name	= Selection
TabIndex	= 2
Top	= 335
Value	= 1 - Checked
Width	= 795

Check3 CheckBox
Caption	= Type
Height	= 290
Index	= 2
Left	= 2200
Name	= Selection
TabIndex	= 3
Top	= 335
Value	= 1 - Checked
Width	= 1052

Check4 CheckBox
Caption	= Quantity
Height	= 290
Index	= 3
Left	= 180
Name	= Selection
TabIndex	= 4
Top	= 700
Value	= 1 - Checked
Width	= 1050

Check5 CheckBox
Caption	= Genre
Height	= 290
Index	= 4
Left	= 1280
Name	= Selection
TabIndex	= 5
Top	= 700
Value	= 1 - Checked
Width	= 875

Command1 CommandButton
Caption   = &OK
Height   = 400
Left   = 1080
Name   = SelectBOK
TabIndex   = 6
Top   = 1440
Width   = 1275

5.5   The Info form, INFO.FRM

The last form in the Music Catalogue project need not
be developed completely from scratch. We shall take
the InfoWindow (INFO.FRM) from the ICONLIST.MAK
project as the basis. We shall make a copy of this.
Choose *Add File* from the *File* menu (Alt-F, D or Ctrl-D)
and load the INFO.FRM file from the \VB_EXMPL
\PICS_TV directory. Open the Project window to check
the result.

In order to include the file in the directory of the current
project, it has to be saved there. Give the command
Save File As from the *File* menu and switch to the
\VB_EXMPL\MC directory. It retains the original filename, INFO.FRM.

Open the InfoWindow to adapt it to the current project.
Delete the *IMouthOpen* and *IMouthShut* icons and the
Timer1 clock. This is done by clicking on them to activate them and then pressing the Del key. Now link the
InfoIcon control to the \VB\ICONS\MISC\MISC31.ICO
file by means of the *Picture* property. Double click on
this property and select the relevant file. Finally,
change the contents of the Label1 box to *Music Catalogue* and the font size to 15.

When the Timer was deleted, only the symbol was
cleared from the work area. The corresponding program code is still present in the form. Open the code
window and activate the *Timer1_Timer* procedure of
the *(general)* object. In the old situation, this code was

linked to the Timer1 object, but in cases where deletion has occurred, Visual Basic allows the 'loose' code to exist as an independent procedure in the general section. This has the advantage that the code is not lost if you delete a control unintentionally. In addition, you can assign the code to a different control. However, we do not need the code in this project so mark all the lines and remove the whole *Timer1_Timer* procedure by pressing Del.

The windows in the Music Catalogue project now contain all the necessary controls. In the next chapter, we shall write the relevant program code.

Exercises

1   Which components make up the structure of a data file?

    _____

2   Describe the structure of the Grid control.

    _____
    _____
    _____

3   What are the differences between an option button and a check box?

    _____
    _____

Answers

1   Which components make up the structure of a data file?

    A data file consists of records which are subdivided into fields.

2   Describe the structure of the Grid control.

The Grid control works as a table with rows and columns. The position of a cell is defined by the co-ordinates of the intersection of a row with a column.

3   What are the differences between an option button and a check box?

Option buttons can be combined into a group in which only one option can be active at any one time. In the case of check boxes, several boxes may be active simultaneously.

6 The Music Catalogue project, writing the program code

Operation of the Music Catalogue data management program takes place entirely via menus. In many cases the execution of menu items depends on the settings of other menu items. In order to make the programming as clear as possible, we shall begin with the menu items which least depend on other menu items.

Double click on the MusicMain form (MAIN.FRM) in the Project window to open the Music Catalogue window if it is not already shown on the screen.

6.1 Programming the menu operation

The HELP menu

The only menu item in the *Help* menu is *Info*. This option is to open the InfoWindow form. The only procedure which Visual Basic provides for activating a menu item is Click. Open the code window for the *Help* menu by clicking on the *Info* menu item. Extend the procedure with the line to activate the InfoWindow form.

```
Sub MInfo_Click (Index As Integer)
    InfoWindow.Show 1
End Sub
```

The EDIT menu

The procedures in the *Edit* menu are all executed in the Mask form. Click on *Edit* in the Music Catalogue form. The code window appears. The procedure to activate the Mask form is as follows:

```
Sub EditMenu_Click ()
    Mask.Show 1
End Sub
```

This menu is not subdivided into menu items. The commands are given in the dialog box which is coded in the Mask form. Accordingly, there is no type declaration for the index of the menu·items in the first line of the procedure. There are no brackets behind the name of this object in the object list.

The VIEW menu

The selection of the required command block is operated within the procedure by means of the value of the index which we assigned to the corresponding menu item in the menu design window. The first menu item has the index 0 and all following menu items have a consecutive index number. Keep in mind that the dividing lines also have an index number. By means of the *Select Case* command, the value of the index determines which element in the structure will be executed.

The *Status line* menu item, with Index=0, serves as a switch: the line is shown or hidden, depending on the status of the menu item. This symmetrical situation is brought about by examining the status of the *Checked* property. MView(0) represents the first item in the *View* menu. Accordingly, the code for the MView_Click procedure is as follows (click on *Status line* to open the code window):

```
Sub MView_Click (Index As Integer)
Select Case Index
    Case 0
        If MView(0).Checked = False Then
            MView(0).Checked = True
            StatusLine.Visible = True
        Else
            MView(0).Checked = False
```

```
                StatusLine.Visible = False
        End If
```

The command block for the *List* of data is analogous:
the index is now 1.

```
    Case 1
        If MView(1).Checked = False Then
            MView(1).Checked = True
            Overview.Visible = True
        Else
            MView(1).Checked = False
            Overview.Visible = False
        End If
```

The *Selection* menu option activates the SelectionList
form (SELECT.FRM) which in turn opens the *Field Selection* dialog box.

```
    Case 3
        SelectionList.Show 1
```

The Common dialog control

The Common dialog control makes it possible to activate a number of standard dialog windows. The type of
dialog window activated depends on the value of the
Action property. (This property is not available in the
design mode and thus not accessible.)

Action value	Description
0	No command
1	Dialog window Open
2	Dialog window Save As
3	Dialog window Color
4	Dialog window Font
5	Dialog window Print
6	Activate the Windows program WINHELP.EXE

The command *CMDialog1.Action=4* in a procedure opens the *Font* dialog window which enables you to choose a font and define the appearance of the text. When the dialog window is closed, the new values of the text parameters must be passed on as current values to the data list.

Each dialog window has the *Flags* property. The value of this property is a combination of constants which represent various parameters. Each parameter has its own specific hexadecimal constant.

Hexadecimal numbers

The hexadecimal system works with sixteen different numerical characters instead of the ten we know from the normal decimal system. The hexadecimal system uses, in addition to the numbers 0 to 9, also the first six capital letters of the alphabet. The letter A corresponds to decimal 10, B to decimal 11 and so on to F which corresponds to decimal 15. The hexadecimal system works analogous to the decimal system: each figure further to the left increases the value of the number at that position by a factor of 16. The most right position represents the single units, the position immediately to the left represents the 'sixteens', the position further to the left represents the '256s' etc. For clarity, hexadecimal numbers are written with the letter h behind them, e.g. 11h (= the decimal 17). Under Windows, and thus under Visual Basic, a decimal number is displayed between the signs &H and &. In the example shown, we shall calculate the value of &H240BF&.

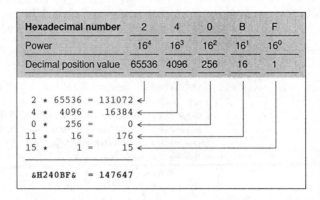

Hexadecimal number	2	4	0	B	F
Power	16^4	16^3	16^2	16^1	16^0
Decimal position value	65536	4096	256	16	1

```
 2 * 65536 = 131072
 4 *  4096 =  16384
 0 *   256 =      0
11 *    16 =    176
15 *     1 =     15
           _____
&H240BF&   = 147647
```

The value of the *Flag* property is the sum of one or
more hexadecimal values just as with the Msg box.
Symbolic constants have been defined for these numbers. In the standard Font dialog box, we shall use the
flags shown below whose names begin with CF_ (for
common font). The flag codes consist of eight numbers
but the pre-zeros can be ignored.

&H00000003& (CF_BOTH) The dialog box shows
             the installed (available) screen and
             printer fonts.

&H00000100& (CF_EFFECTS) Adds check boxes
             for Strikthru and Underline to the di-
             alog box, and provides the Color
             options list. The manual and the
             Help texts incorrectly show the
             value &H200& for this function. This
             value belongs to CF_APPLY.

&H00008000& (CF_WYSIWYG) The font lists con-
             tain only fonts which are available
             for both screen and printer.

&H00020000& (CF_SCALABLEONLY) Restricts
             the selection to scalable fonts only.

             _____ +

&H00028103&

The value which has been calculated in this way is used to define the layout of the standard Font dialog window.

```
Case 4
    CMDialog1.Flags = &H28103&
    CMDialog1.Action = 4
    Overview.FontName = CMDialog1.FontName
    Overview.FontSize = CMDialog1.FontSize
    Overview.FontBold = CMDialog1.FontBold
    Overview.FontItalic =
        CMDialog1.FontItalic
    Overview.FontUnderline =
        CMDialog1.FontUnderline
    Overview.FontStrikethru =
        CMDialog1.FontStrikethru
    Overview.ForeColor = CMDialog1.Color
```

The value of the *Flags* property may also be assigned as a combination with the logical operator *Or.*

```
&H3& Or &H100& Or &H8000& Or &H20000&
```

If a menu item also has a submenu, that submenu is automatically opened by a click. Accordingly, we do not need to write a code for *Case 5* (the *Point size*).

The activation of the Background colour dialog window requires the following commands:

```
Case 6
    CMDialog1.Action = 3
    Overview.BackColor = CMDialog1.Color
End Select
End Sub
```

The standard dialog window automatically contains the *Cancel* command button. Our program will have to determine if the window has been closed due to activation of the *Cancel* button (in contrast to being closed with confirmation of new values). In that case, the rest of the Case structure code should not be executed. We can ensure this by means of an error-handling routine. The *Cancel/Error=True* property results in the Common Dialog control generating the specific error code 32755 via the *Cancel* button.

In the Properties window, adjust the *CancelError* property of CMDialog1 to True, and place the following command in the MView_Click procedure in front of the *Select Case Index* command:

```
On Error GoTo ErrCanc
```

Conclude the error-handling routine after *End Select* with the lines:

```
ErrCanc:
    Exit Sub
```

In the *Point size* submenu, the code has the same structure as in the MView_Click procedure:

```
Sub MLetter_Click (Index As Integer)
Select Case Index
    Case 0
        Overview.FontSize = 8
    Case 1
        Overview.FontSize = 10
    Case 2
        Overview.FontSize = 12
    Case 3
        Overview.FontSize = 14
    End Select
End Sub
```

Save the result and test the current version of the program. The program will halt at menu items for which no program code has been written as yet. You can start it up again by pressing Alt-R, R or Shift-F5 if you wish to examine another menu item.

Default values for menu options

When the program is run, it is not necessary to provide all the commands in the menus. This depends on the situation. For instance, at the start of the program, there may be no data file in memory; in that case, it is no use showing options which can only be implemented when a file has been loaded. This applies in particular to the options *List, Selection, Font, Point size* and *Background colour* from the *View* menu and to the *Edit* menu. Accordingly, you should assign the value False to the *Enabled* property in the Menu Design window, in other words, remove the cross from the Enabled check box.

The FILE menu

The procedures involving files are activated from the *File* menu. In order to be able to end the program in a correct and orderly way, we shall add the *End* command to the Case structure of the menu. This is done under *Case 7*. This procedure will also deal with the exit from a standard dialog window via the *Cancel* button by means of an error-handling routine with On Error. Ensure that the label for the error routine is different to that which dealt with the previous error-handling routine (in the *View* menu).

The command blocks for the other Case values will be dealt with shortly.

```
Sub MFile_Click (Index As Integer)
On Error GoTo MisCanc
    Select Case Index
        Case 0

        Case 1

        Case 2
```

```
            Case 3

            Case 5

            Case 7
                  End
        End Select
    MisCanc:
        Exit Sub
    End Sub
```

6.2   The structure and management of the file

Modules in file management

The file management model which we shall apply in our program covers the following main components:

- the disk on which the file is stored
- the file with all records which is in memory
- a copy of the current record
- the input mask containing the fields of the current record
- an empty record for making new records and deleting an existing record.

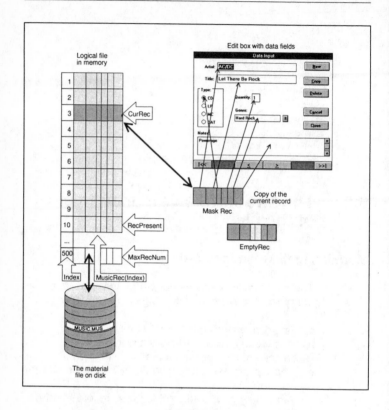

The file structure in memory

The file we are going to create is subdivided into *records*. The contents of a record encompass one sound device in our example, or a set of sound devices which belong together (such as a double CD). Each record is divided into the *data fields* Artists, Title, Type, Quantity, Genre and Notes. The following table gives a summary of the features of these data fields.

Name	Type	Length
Artist	String	30
Title	String	30
Type	Integer	
Quantity	String	2
Genre	String	15
Notes	String	200

In Visual Basic, the two values for the name and the type of data field can be combined to form a *new data type*. In our program, we shall give the name Record to this new data type. Because this data type is to be available all through the project, it must be declared globally. We shall make a global module for this.

Create the new module, Module1.bas using the *New Module* command from the *File* menu (Alt-F, M). Save the new module under the name GLOBAL.BAS. Also save the project in its current state.

A data type is declared by means of the *Type* command. Place the declarations shown below in the GLOBAL.BAS file:

```
Type Record
    Artist As String * 30
    Title As String * 30
    Type As Integer
    Quantity As String * 2
    Genre As String * 15
    Notes As String * 200
End Type
```

All data in the music catalogue must be located in memory. Because Visual Basic cannot dynamically manage unlimited files, we must specify the maximum number of records in the file. We shall use the randomly chosen number of 500. The theoretical maximum is 32,767 since a constant is automatically declared using the Integer type.

We shall define the maximum number of records using the *MaxRecNum* global constant. Values which do not change during the execution of the program are stored in constants. In Visual Basic, a constant is declared using the *Const* command. The declaration must be made before the constant is used in the program: therefore we shall include this command in the GLOBAL.BAS module.

```
Global Const MaxRecNum = 500
```

We can now reserve space in memory for the records in the file according to size and arrangement. We use the *MusicRec(MaxRecNum)* command to create 500 empty records in memory. Visual Basic reserves the necessary memory for these. A specific record is addressed by means of its index number. This method makes it possible to manipulate a complete record in the program without having to load and save individual fields.

```
Global MusicRec(MaxRecNum) As Record
```

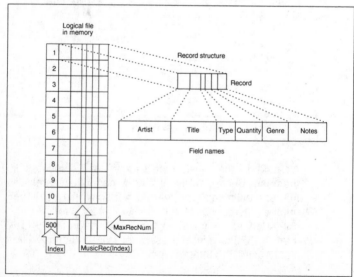

Creating a new file

In a completely new file, no record has yet been filled. Later, the program must be able to find out how many records out of the possible MaxRecNum have been actually filled. This value is stored in the *RecPresent* global variable. In addition, because we wish to be able to browse through the file, the last record need not be by definition the current record. The *CurRec* variable contains the index number of the current record.

```
Global RecPresent As Integer
Global CurRec As Integer
```

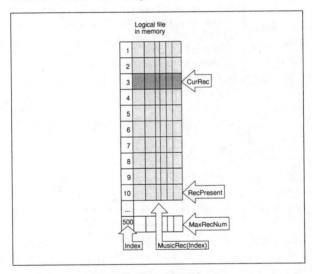

The *Index* variable makes it possible to address a specific record in the file. Accordingly, all management parameters are assigned a standard beginning value in the new music file. We assign the value 1 to the *RecPresent* and *CurRec* variables to be able to start managing the records, otherwise the program will not be able to start up. We must ensure that the first record is empty. Accordingly, we shall create a record in which the fields are empty. It is given the name EmptyRec.

```
Global EmptyRec As Record
```

We shall create the empty record using the Empty-Rec_Create global procedure. We leave most data fields empty in this procedure. Type is given the value 0 and Quantity the default value 1.

We shall place the new EmptyRec_Create procedure in the GLOBAL.BAS module by means of the *New Procedure* command from the *View* menu (Alt-V, N). A dialog window appears. Make sure that Sub is active and type the name: EmptyRec_Create.

```
Sub EmptyRec_Create ()
    EmptyRec.Artist = ""
    EmptyRec.Title = ""
    EmptyRec.Type = 0
    EmptyRec.Quantity = "1"
    EmptyRec.Genre = ""
    EmptyRec.Notes = ""
End Sub
```

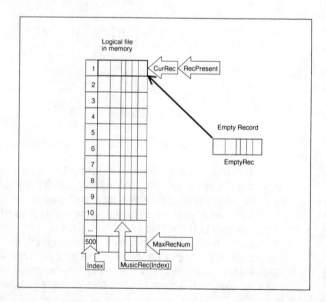

The EmptyRec_Create procedure is executed only once during the program in order to create the Empty-Rec empty record. This takes place immediately the MusicMain basic form is opened. Extend the Form_Load procedure in the MusicMain form with the line which activates the EmptyRec_Create global procedure.

```
Sub Form_Load ()
    EmptyRec_Create
End Sub
```

Note: We could have included the code for the Empty-Rec_Create procedure in the Form_Load procedure. But we have centralised the code for the file management in the GLOBAL.BAS module because this provides the advantage that we can easily adopt this code as a whole into another project by copying the GLOBAL.BAS module.

After this small excursion to the construction of Empty-Rec, we shall return to the initialization of the file. The file in memory must be brought into the original undeveloped state when the command *New* is given from the *File* menu. Firstly, the *RecPresent* and *CurRec* variables are assigned the value 1 and this record is filled with a copy of the EmptyRec empty record. Subsequently, the Mask input form is activated so that the first record can be filled with data. To do all this, add the following commands to the MFile_Click procedure code at *Case 0* in the MAIN.FRM code window:

```
Sub MFile_Click (Index As Integer)
    ...
        Case 0
            RecPresent = 1
            CurRec = 1
            MusicRec(1) = EmptyRec
            Mask.Show 1
    ...
End Sub
```

Because we always deal with the currently active record in the input mask, we shall create a copy of the current record in the *MaskRec* buffer variable. We edit this copy in the input mask without the original data of the file being lost. If we were to write the data directly to the file, the original data would be lost immediately. In that case, any alterations could not be cancelled.

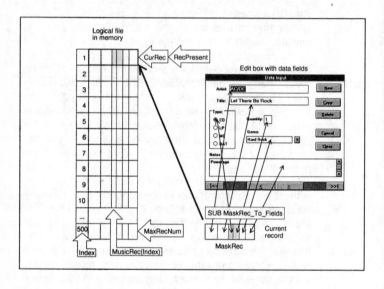

Extend the declaration part of GLOBAL.BAS by adding the line:

```
Global MaskRec As Record
```

When the Mask form is activated, the contents of the current record in memory must be copied to the *Mask-Rec* variable. This takes place in the Form_Load procedure. The contents of the fields of the *MaskRec* variable are assigned to the relevant controls in the Mask form. We shall write the MaskRec_To_Fields global procedure for this in the MASK.FRM code window (we shall return to this shortly):

```
Sub Form_Load ()
    MaskRec = MusicRec(CurRec)
    MaskRec_To_Fields
End Sub
```

In the declaration of the Record data type, we defined the maximum field length. If the data occupy less space, the other characters in the field should be converted to spaces. If we then edit the contents of the field further, the string or the number always has the maximum length. With the exception of the Type record field (always only one character), all record fields are checked for unnecessary spaces. The *RTrim$* function removes the spaces from the end of a string.

The four option buttons in the Type data field have the indices 0 to 3. Due to the nature of the data, only one option may be active at any one time. This means that the index of the chosen option is also the value in the record field. We shall set the value of the *Value* property of this control to True via the index of the currently active option button. This property is then set to False for the other three option buttons.

In a global procedure, if the procedure is going to change a property of an operational element, it is necessary to specify the exact location of the element. This specification is made by typing the name of the property, preceded by the *name of the element and a dot.*

In the following stage of writing the program code, we shall use the *New Procedure* option from the *View* menu (Alt-V, N) to write the MaskRec_To_Fields global procedure and its counterpart, Fields_To_MaskRec. Add the following subroutines to the code window of GLOBAL.BAS.

```
Sub MaskRec_To_Fields ()
    Mask.MaskArtist.Text =
↺      RTrim$(MaskRec.Artist)
    Mask.MaskTitle.Text =
↺      RTrim$(MaskRec.Title)
```

```
        Mask.MaskOption(MaskRec.Type).Value = True
        Mask.MaskQuantity.Text =
⇨           RTrim$(MaskRec.Quantity)
        Mask.MaskGenre.Text =
⇨           RTrim$(MaskRec.Genre)
        Mask.MaskNotes.Text =
⇨           RTrim$(MaskRec.Notes)
End Sub
```

The reverse process copies the contents of the operating elements in the input mask to the fields of the *MaskRec* variable. The *LTrim$()* function removes any unintentionally typed spaces at the beginning of the input.

Here too, the Type field receives exceptional treatment: the program uses a loop to examine which option button has been activated. Then the index of this button is copied to the Type field in the record. Create a new procedure in GLOBAL.BAS as previously.

```
Sub Fields_To_MaskRec ()
    MaskRec.Artist =
⇨        LTrim$(Mask.MaskArtist.Text)
    MaskRec.Title =
⇨        LTrim$(Mask.MaskTitle.Text)
    For TypeIndex = 0 To 3
        If Mask.MaskOption(TypeIndex).Value =
⇨              True Then
              MaskRec.Type = TypeIndex
    End If
    Next TypeIndex
    MaskRec.Quantity =
⇨        LTrim$(Mask.MaskQuantity.Text)
    MaskRec.Genre = LTrim$(Mask.MaskGenre.Text)
    MaskRec.Notes =
⇨        LTrim$(Mask.MaskNotes.Text)
End Sub
```

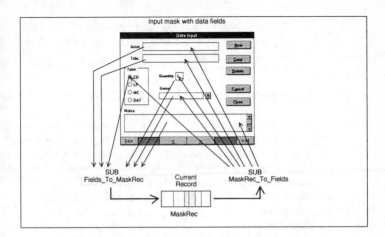

Input mask with data fields

The Genre Combo box provides a list of standard music categories in addition to space for free text input. This standard list is created by adding a number of registrations to the existing empty list by means of the *Add-Item* property when the Mask form is loaded. Open the code window for MASK.FRM.

```
Sub Form_Load ()
    MaskRec = MusicRec(CurRec)
    MaskRec_To_Fields
    MaskGenre.AddItem "Rock"
    MaskGenre.AddItem "Pop"
    MaskGenre.AddItem "Blues"
    MaskGenre.AddItem "Jazz"
    MaskGenre.AddItem "Heavy Metal"
    MaskGenre.AddItem "Funk"
    MaskGenre.AddItem "Classical"
...
End Sub
```

Depending on your own taste, you can add or exclude genres. The program listing in Appendix C registers the following categories in addition to those shown above: Folk, Hoompapa, Country, Rap, World Music, Hard Rock, Punk, Soundtrack, Swing, Synthesizer, Reggae, House, Techno, Disco, Soft Rock, Rock 'n Roll, Modern Serious, Trash Metal, Experimental, Foot and Mouth, Unknown. The *Sorted=True* property places the added items in alphabetical order.

6.3   Procedures in the Mask form

In the initial situation, we have a file with an empty record in memory. In this copy of the file, records are created, copied and deleted. There are four command buttons which enable you to browse forwards and backwards through the records and to jump to the beginning and end of the file. The *Cancel* and *Close* buttons have special significance because they close the input mask.

The NEW command button

The *New* command button procedure first checks if there is enough space in the file for a new record. If so, the Artist field must contain at least one character that is not a space after input has been made: only then is the input valid. The validity check first removes all beginning and end spaces by means of the *Trim$()* function.

When the above demands for a new record have been met, the contents of the operating elements (controls) are copied to the buffer record (1 in the diagram below) by the Fields_To_Mask procedure. Subsequently, this record is copied to the file in memory: MusicRec(Cur-Rec)=MaskRec (step 2). When the data of the existing record have been saved, the procedure continues with the preparation of the data for the new record. The RecPresent counter is increased (3) and the new value is assigned to the record number CurRec (4). A new record always receives the next consecutive free record number. The current record is filled with the contents of the EmptyRec empty record (5) and its fields are copied to the fields in the input mask by the MaskRec_To_Fields procedure (6).

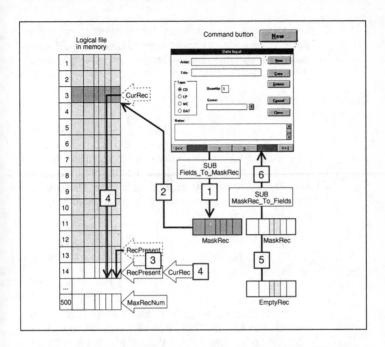

Open the MaskBNew object in the MASK.FRM code window or double click on the *New* button in the Mask form (caption: Data Input).

```
Sub MaskBNew_Click ()
    If RecPresent < MaxRecNum Then
        If Trim$(MaskArtist.Text) <> "" Then
            Fields_To_MaskRec
            MusicRec(CurRec) = MaskRec
            RecPresent = RecPresent + 1
            CurRec = RecPresent
            MaskRec = EmptyRec
            MaskRec_To_Fields
```

If the check shows that the Artist data field is empty, we have no valid record. The program will react by displaying an error message which indicates what has gone wrong. Because an incomplete record can only occur within the Mask form, we shall create a *local procedure* with the name Rec_Incomp. This procedure will be activated in the Else branch of the MaskBNew_Click procedure. (We shall describe the creation of this procedure shortly.)

```
Else
     Rec_Incomp
End If
```

The outer Else branch will be executed if all records have been filled (this quantity has been defined via MaxRecNum). Nothing can be done about this, except simply deleting existing records; thus an error message will be sufficient.

```
Else
     MsgBox "There are no more available
↳          records.", 48
End If
```

After each alteration, the counters for the current record and the number of filled records have to be brought up to date. These values are displayed in the status line of the MusicMain form. Because the counter numbers can be changed in many procedures, we shall create a global procedure to keep the status line up to date (we shall describe writing this global procedure in detail shortly). Now add the following line to the MaskBNew subroutine under the last End If.

```
StatusLine_Modify
```

With a new record, at least the name of the artist has to be entered, otherwise the record is not valid. Accordingly, we shall accentuate the Artist field in the input mask. The *SetFocus* property marks the contents of the field which is activated for input. Add the following line to the code.

```
MaskArtist.SetFocus
End Sub
```

Finally, the two independent procedures mentioned have to be written.

In the StatusLine_Modify global procedure, we shall replace the initial value of the *Caption* (Record:) property by this string plus information about the number of the current record and the number of records present. Place this procedure in the GLOBAL.BAS module (via *View, New Procedure*).

```
Sub StatusLine_Modify ()
    MusicMain.StatusRec.Caption = "Record: "
⇨       + Str$(CurRec) + " of " +
⇨       Str$(RecPresent)
End Sub
```

The second independent procedure is a part of the Mask form. Because this procedure is local and does not depend on the results of other procedures, we shall place this procedure in the general part *(general)* of the Mask form. Open the Mask form code window and create the Rec_Incomp procedure by selecting the *New Procedure* option from the *View* menu (Alt-V, N).

```
Sub Rec_Incomp ()
    MsgBox "Incomplete record." + Chr$(13) +
⇨          "Enter the name of the artist.", 48
        MaskArtist.SetFocus
End Sub
```

Save the result and now try out the *New* command button.

The COPY command button

The Copy command creates a new record which is a copy of the current record. This saves typework at input if the name of the artist and the genre remain the same.

In copying, the method of working is almost identical to that in creating a new record. But because the previous contents have to remain intact, we do not make the current record empty by activating a copy of the Empty-Rec empty record; therefore the two commands needed to do this can be dispensed with.

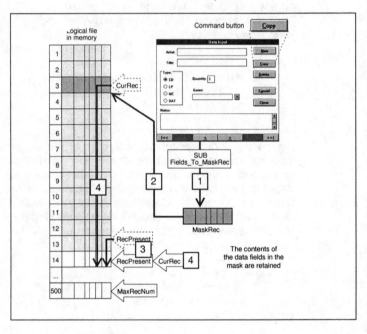

Add the following lines to the MaskBCopy subroutine in the MASK.FRM code window:

```
Sub MaskBCopy_Click ()
    If RecPresent < MaxRecNum Then
        If Trim$(MaskArtist.Text) <> "" Then
            Fields_To_MaskRec
            MusicRec(CurRec) = MaskRec
            RecPresent = RecPresent + 1
            CurRec = RecPresent
            MaskRec_To_Fields
```

```
        Else
            Rec_Incomp
        End If
    Else
        MsgBox "There are no more available
            records.", 48
    End If
    StatusLine_Modify
    MaskArtist.SetFocus
End Sub
```

The DELETE command button

Before dealing with the code for actually deleting a
record, we shall create a *safeguard against unintentional deletion*. The *MsgBox()* function can not only display a message, it can also contain command buttons
and convey the code of the activated button to the program. In our example we shall add the *Yes* and *No* buttons (type 36), which produce the codes 6 and 7. We
shall assign these values to the *Choice* variable. Only if
Choice=6 will deletion of the current record actually
take place.

```
Sub MaskBDelete_Click ()
    Choice = MsgBox("Do you really want to
        delete the record?", 36)
    If Choice = 6 Then
```

There are three situations in which you can delete a
record:

1   The file consists of only one record.

In this case, only the data fields in the mask (3)
and those in the current record (2) need to be filled
with the contents of the fields from EmptyRec (1):

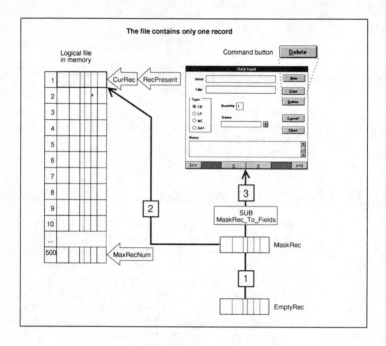

```
If RecPresent = 1 Then
    MaskRec = EmptyRec
    MusicRec(CurRec) = MaskRec
    MaskRec_To_Fields
```

2   The record to be deleted is the last one in the file.

In this case too, the last completed record is filled with the contents of the fields from EmptyRec (1). This is also done with the corresponding record in the music file (2). When the pointer to the last completed record (3) and the pointer to the current record (4) have been decreased by one, we can extract the current record (5) from the music file and copy the fields from the buffer record to the data fields in the mask (6).

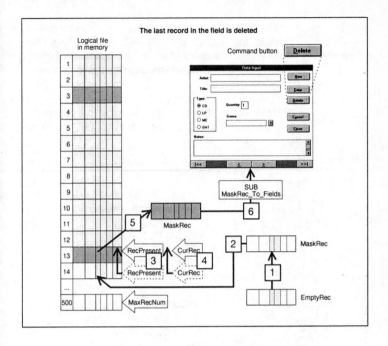

The last record in the field is deleted

```
Else
    If CurRec = RecPresent Then
        MaskRec = EmptyRec
        MusicRec(CurRec) = MaskRec
        RecPresent = RecPresent - 1
        CurRec = RecPresent
        MaskRec = MusicRec(CurRec)
        MaskRec_To_Fields
```

3 The record to be deleted is not at the end of the file.

If the music file contains more than one record and if the record to be deleted is not at the end of the file, there will be at least one more record after the record in question. After deletion has taken place, the following records must all move up a place. A counter loop will shift all appropriate records to the record number which is one less than their current number (1a to 1g in the diagram). Then we shall delete the last record (step 2) and decrease the pointer to the last record by one (step 3). Finally, the fields in the buffer record (4) and in the mask (5) are activated.

In all three cases, the procedure brings the status line up to date, and the text cursor moves to the Artist input field.

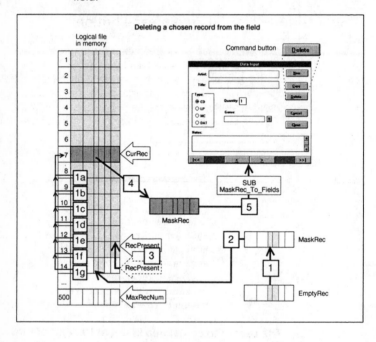

```
                Else
                    For RecNr = CurRec To
⇨                            RecPresent - 1
                        MusicRec(RecNr) =
⇨                            MusicRec(RecNr + 1)
                    Next RecNr
                    MaskRec = EmptyRec
                    MusicRec(RecPresent) = MaskRec
                    RecPresent = RecPresent - 1
```

```
                    MaskRec = MusicRec(CurRec)
                    MaskRec_To_Fields
                End If
            End If
        End If
        StatusLine_Modify
        MaskArtist.SetFocus
End Sub
```

The BEGINNING OF FILE command button

The command button |<< moves the program to the beginning of the data file: CurRec=1 (step 3 in the diagram). Subsequently, the first record is displayed (4 and 5). However, this may only take place if the current record satisfies the requirements. Prior to the jump to the beginning, the contents of the mask (1) are stored in the file (2).

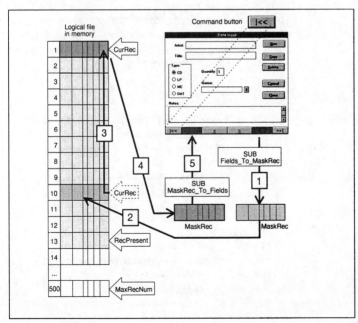

```
Sub MaskBRBegin_Click ()
    If Trim$(MaskArtist.Text) <> "" Then
        Fields_To_MaskRec
        MusicRec(CurRec) = MaskRec
        CurRec = 1
        MaskRec = MusicRec(CurRec)
        MaskRec_To_Fields
    Else
        Rec_Incomp
    End If
    StatusLine_Modify
End Sub
```

The BROWSE BACKWARDS button

A click on the < command button should display the
previous record in the mask: CurRec=CurRec-1 (step 3
in the diagram). This can only take place if there actually is a previous record, in other words, if the current
record number is greater than 1. If not, an appropriate
error message should be displayed. Prior to the next
record (4) being loaded in the mask (5), the current
contents (1) should be saved (2).

```
Sub MaskBRPrevious_Click ()
    If CurRec > 1 Then
        If Trim$(MaskArtist.Text) <> "" Then
            Fields_To_MaskRec
            MusicRec(CurRec) = MaskRec
            CurRec = CurRec - 1
            MaskRec = MusicRec(CurRec)
            MaskRec_To_Fields
        Else
            Rec_Incomp
        End If
    Else
        Msgbox "Beginning of the file.", 64
    End If
    StatusLine_Modify
End Sub
```

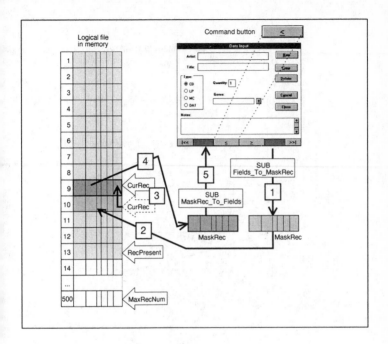

The BROWSE FORWARDS button

One click on the > command button should display the next record in the mask: CurRec=CurRec+1 (step 3 in the diagram overleaf). If the end of the file has not been reached, in other words, if the current record number is smaller than the number of records present, the next record will be able to be shown (steps 4 and 5). If the end of the file has been reached, the program generates an error message.

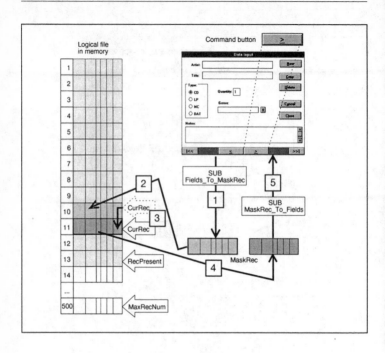

```
Sub MaskBRNext_Click ()
    If CurRec < RecPresent Then
        If Trim$(MaskArtist.Text) <> "" Then
            Fields_To_MaskRec
            MusicRec(CurRec) = MaskRec
            CurRec = CurRec + 1
            MaskRec = MusicRec(CurRec)
            MaskRec_To_Fields
        Else
            Rec_Incomp
        End If
    Else
            Msgbox "End of file.", 64
    End If
    StatusLine_Modify
End Sub
```

The END OF FILE command button

The program will jump to the end of the file via the >>|
command button: CurRec=RecPresent (3 in the diagram).

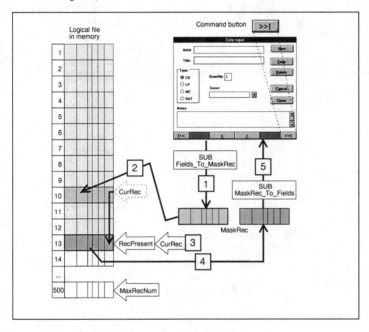

```
Sub MaskBREnd_Click ()
    If Trim$(MaskArtist.Text) <> "" Then
        Fields_To_MaskRec
        MusicRec(CurRec) = MaskRec
        CurRec = RecPresent
        MaskRec = MusicRec(CurRec)
        MaskRec_To_Fields
    Else
        Rec_Incomp
    End If
    StatusLine_Modify
End Sub
```

The CANCEL command button

The *Cancel* command button enables you to leave the mask without saving the values in the current record. If no artist has been specified in a *new* record, this record will be ignored in any case. A test will be applied in which, in an IF structure, two statements will be linked to one another by means of the *And* logical operator. This means that the test can only have a positive outcome if both statements are true. When the *Or* logical operator is applied, the condition is satisfied if one of the statements is true.

Each time we quit the mask by means of the *Cancel* or *Close* buttons, the program is to sort the records in alphabetical order according to the Artist field. We shall write the Sort_Artist global procedure for this (given in detail shortly).

First the procedure for the *Cancel* command button:

```
Sub MaskBCancel_Click ()
    MousePointer = 11
    If (Trim$(MaskArtist.Text) = "")
↳        And (CurRec = RecPresent) Then
        RecPresent = RecPresent - 1
        CurRec = RecPresent
    End If
    Sort_Artist
    StatusLine_Modify
    Unload Mask
    MousePointer = 0
End Sub
```

The CLOSE command button

The *Close* command should be given after concluding work within the records. The program procedure has to check whether or not the current record is valid. If not, it should be completed correctly or deleted, otherwise the procedure will not be finalised. The current con-

tents of the data fields (1 in the diagram) are copied to
the file (2) if the current record is valid at the closure of
the input mask.

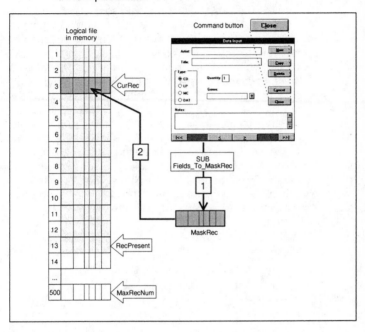

```
Sub MaskBClose_Click ()
    MousePointer = 11
    If Trim$(MaskArtist.Text) <> "" Then
        Fields_To_MaskRec
        MusicRec(CurRec) = MaskRec
        Sort_Artist
        Unload Mask
    Else
        Rec_Incomp
    End If
    StatusLine_Modify
    MousePointer = 0
End Sub
```

Sorting the records

The records are stored in alphabetical order in the music file. The Artist field is the sole sorting criterion. For this sorting process, we shall use a simple algorithm which is based on a triangular exchange. The program searches through the entire list checking if the next name should be placed in front of the current name. If so, the two records are switched. The file is run through as many times as is necessary until no further switching is necessary. The *SortFlag* variable indicates whether records have been switched in a runthrough. Prior to each runthrough, the *SortFlag* variable is given the value False; after an exchange the value becomes True. A test of the current value determines whether another runthrough is to take place. After a runthrough without switching, the value of the *SortFlag* variable will remain False, indicating that the file is completely sorted.

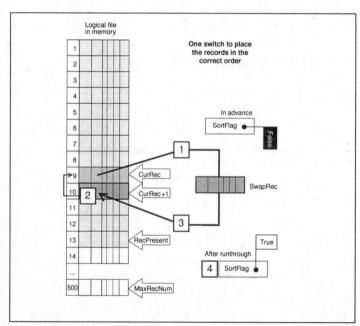

The contents of two records can only be placed in the correct order by means of a third record, the buffer record called SwapRec. This record is also of the self-defined Record data type. Declare the new global variable in GLOBAL.BAS.

```
Global SwapRec As Record
```

Variables which are declared using *Dim* within a procedure are only available as local variables within that procedure. In contrast, variables declared using *Dim* in the general part of a form are available for all procedures in that form.

This sorting procedure is to be a global procedure. Select *New Procedure* from the *View* menu and give it the name Sort_Artist.

```
Sub Sort_Artist ()
Dim SortFlag As Integer
    If RecPresent > 1 Then
```

The Do-Loop-Until loop structure

The Do-Loop-Until structure is operated by the result of the command block. Only after the command block has been carried out does the program examine whether the condition after *Until* has been fulfilled. This means that the loop will always be executed at least once.

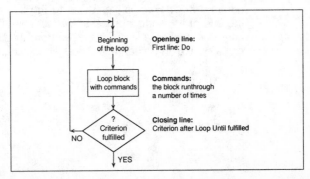

```
Do
    MousePointer = 11
    SortFlag = False
```

The loop with the RecNr counter checks the entire list
and compares the name of the artist in the current
record (RecNr) with the name of the artist in the following record (RecNr+1). The final value of the counter
may not be larger than the number of records minus
one. The final comparison deals with the penultimate
and the ultimate records. If the loop were to be contin-
ued through to RecPresent, there would be no record
available for comparison with the last record. Therefore, the loop is ended when RecNr= RecPresent-1.

```
        For RecNr = 1 To RecPresent - 1
            If Trim$(MusicRec(RecNr).Artist)
↻                > Trim$(MusicRec(RecNr
↻                + 1).Artist) Then
                SwapRec = MusicRec(RecNr)
                MusicRec(RecNr) =
↻                    MusicRec(RecNr + 1)
                MusicRec(RecNr + 1) = SwapRec
                SortFlag = True
            End If
        Next RecNr
    Loop Until SortFlag = False
End If
```

If the file has to be sorted because a record has to be
added, the *CurRec* pointer is set to the last record at
the end of the sorting process. But because it is more
convenient when a list is displayed from the beginning
onwards, we shall change the pointer position.

```
    If CurRec = RecPresent Then
        CurRec = 1
    End If
    MousePointer = 0
End Sub
```

Marking the contents of a field

Just as in many other Windows applications, we wish to be able to mark the contents of the current field in our program too. This makes it possible, among other things, to delete the entire contents with one key if required.

The number of marked characters is stored in the *Sel-Length* property. The number of characters in the *Text* property string is calculated by means of the *Len()* function. The initial position for marking is defined using the *SelStart* property. The GotFocus event procedure is executed when a control has become activated by a click or by means of the Tab key.

Create the following new procedures in MASK.FRM using *View, New Procedure.*

```
Sub MaskArtist_GotFocus ()
    MaskArtist.SelStart = 0
    MaskArtist.SelLength = Len(MaskArtist.Text)
End Sub

Sub MaskTitle_GotFocus ()
    MaskTitle.SelStart = 0
    MaskTitle.SelLength = Len(MaskTitle.Text)
End Sub

Sub MaskQuantity_GotFocus ()
    MaskQuantity.SelStart = 0
    MaskQuantity.SelLength = Len(MaskQuantity.Text)
End Sub

Sub MaskGenre_GotFocus ()
    MaskGenre.SelStart = 0
    MaskGenre.SelLength = Len(MaskGenre.Text)
End Sub
```

```
Sub MaskNotes_GotFocus ()
    MaskNotes.SelStart = 0
    MaskNotes.SelLength = Len(MaskNotes.Text)
End Sub
```

6.4   Saving and loading a data file

To avoid losing the entered data when you switch off
the computer, the file in memory should be written to
disk.

The SAVE AS menu item

The *Save As* menu option opens the standard *Save
File As* dialog window.

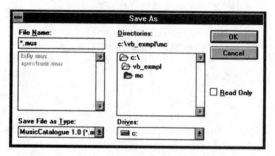

If all files with a music catalogue were to have the extension MUS, it would be more easy to recognize these
files. We can arrange this by assigning the value MUS
to the *DefaultExt* property. This property contains the
extension which will be assigned to each file name if no
other extension is specified. The text box under File
Name then displays *.mus* and Visual Basic adds this
extension to the name which you now enter unless you
specify otherwise.

In the combination window in the two dialog windows
Save and *Open*, there is an options list of possible extensions. We can compile this list by means of the *Fil-*

ter property. A registration in the *Filter* property consists of a descriptive text and the corresponding extension. An extension must be accompanied by the symbol | at both the beginning and the end of the extension. If you specify more than one filter, you can use the *FilterIndex* property to determine which registration in the list is to be the default value. The first registration has the index 1.

Change the properties in the CMDialog1 control in the MusicMain form as we outlined above. These data influence both the *Save File As* and the *Open* dialog windows.

CMDialog1 CommonDialog
DefaultExt   = mus
Filter   = MusicCatalogue 1.0 (*.mus)|*.mus|
⇨   All files (*.*)|*.*|
FilterIndex   = 1

We have already seen that a dialog window is opened via the *Action* property. Go to the *Case 3* section in the MFile_Click subroutine in the code window of MAIN.FRM.

```
Sub MFile_Click (Index As Integer)
. . .
        Case 3
              CMDialog1.Action = 2
              Memory_To_Disk
. . .
End Sub
```

The Common dialog control generates a standard window and parameters to convey values. We shall have to write the program code ourselves, in this case the code to save a data file. Accordingly, we shall write the global procedure Memory_To_Disk.

The *Open* command opens an information channel between memory and disk. The first parameter of the instruction is the path plus a file name; this information is obtained from the *Filename* property of CMDialog1. Whether the data are to be written (*Output*) or read (*Input*) is specified behind the instruction *For* in the code. In the structure used here, the *Open* command ends with the allocation of a file number (*As #1*). Each opened file must have a unique number (#n). Since we only manage one file in our program, this number will be 1. It is necessary to specify this number in each read or write command so that the program will know to which file the command refers.

Open the GLOBAL.BAS code window and create the new procedure (*View, New Procedure*).

```
Sub Memory_To_Disk ()
    MousePointer = 11
    Open MusicMain.CMDialog1.Filename
⇨         For Output As #1
```

The *Print #n* command writes data in a *sequential file*. In order to be able to easily recognize files as a music catalogue, we shall write the string 'MC1.00' in each file first. The semi-colon at the end of the command prevents the data being followed by the CHR$(13) character (Carriage Return) as the separator. This will mean that the data are stored more compactly. The *RecPresent* variable indicates the number of records in the file. This information makes it easier to load the file later.

```
    Print #1, "MC1.00";
    Print #1, RecPresent;
```

A loop of the For-Next type enables the program to write all records in the file according to the specified structure.

```
    For RecNr = 1 To RecPresent
        Print #1, MusicRec(RecNr).Artist;
        Print #1, MusicRec(RecNr).Title;
        Print #1, MusicRec(RecNr).Type;
```

```
        Print #1, MusicRec(RecNr).Quantity;
        Print #1, MusicRec(RecNr).Genre;
        Print #1, MusicRec(RecNr).Notes;
    Next RecNr
```

The *Close* command closes the file with the specified number; in our example, that is file #1.

```
    Close #1
```

Activating the StatusLine_Modify procedure ensures that the filename, which has just become known, is now shown in the status line. The restoration of the shape of the mouse pointer forms the last command in the Memory_To_Disk procedure.

```
    StatusLine_Modify
    MousePointer = 0
End Sub
```

The display of the filename in the status line has not yet been coded in the StatusLine_Modify procedure. We shall import this information in the *Caption* property of the StatusFile control. Up until now only the *Record:* string is located there. The new command adds the path and filename, both in capital letters (UCase$). Add the following lines shown in boldface to the Status-Line_Modify procedure in the GLOBAL.BAS code window.

```
Sub StatusLine_Modify ()
    MusicMain.StatusFile.Caption = "File: "
↳        + UCase$(MusicMain.CMDialog1.Filename)
    MusicMain.StatusRecord.Caption = "Record: "
↳        + Str$(CurRec) + " of "
↳        + Str$(RecPresent)
End Sub
```

The OPEN menu item

The *Open* menu item opens the standard *Open* dialog box.

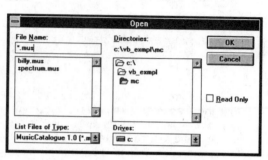

The file is accessible via the Disk_To_Memory global procedure which is now added to the MFile_Click sub-routine in the MAIN.FRM code window.

```
Sub MFile_Click (Index As Integer)
...
        Case 1
            CMDialog1.Action = 1
            Disk_To_Memory
...
End Sub
```

In contrast to the Memory_To_Disk global procedure in which *Output* is used for saving the file, the Disk_To_Memory global procedure uses *Input* to load a file from disk. Create the Disk_To_Memory procedure in GLOBAL.BAS (*View, New Procedure*).

```
Sub Disk_To_Memory ()
    MousePointer = 11
    Open MusicMain.CMDialog1.Filename
        For Input As #1
```

We shall first check if the file to be loaded has been created using the Music Catalogue program. To do this, we shall use the *Input$()* function to read the first six characters in the file and this string is compared to our MC1.00 code. If there is no correspondence, an error message will appear. The incorrect file is then neatly closed by means of the *Close* command and the procedure is concluded with Exit Sub.

```
If Input$(6, #1) <> "MC1.00" Then
    MsgBox "File cannot be loaded."
          + Chr$(13) + "INCORRECT FILE
          FORMAT", 48
    Close #1
    Exit Sub
End If
```

Subsequently, the program reads the number of records using the *Input* function. This function imports the contents of the file according to the data of the specified variable. Because the *RecPresent* and *Music-Rec().Type* variables are of the Integer data type, they can simply be loaded by means of the *Input* command. When using the *Input$()* function, you must always specify the number of characters in question; the string which has been read is assigned to the specified variable.

```
Input #1, RecPresent
For RecNr = 1 To RecPresent
    MusicRec(RecNr).Artist = Input$(30, #1)
    MusicRec(RecNr).Title = Input$(30, #1)
    Input #1, MusicRec(RecNr).Type
    MusicRec(RecNr).Quantity =
          Input$(2, #1)
    MusicRec(RecNr).Genre = Input$(15, #1)
    MusicRec(RecNr).Notes = Input$(200, #1)
Next RecNr
```

When the disk file has been closed, the *CurRec* record pointer returns to the first record.

```
          Close #1
          CurRec = 1
          StatusLine_Modify
          MousePointer = 0
End Sub
```

The SAVE menu item

The *Save* menu item writes the file to disk without first requesting the name. But if you give this command before a name has been specified, the *Save File As* dialog window has to be opened. The test examines the value of the *Filename* property to see whether or not a path and/or filename has been specified. Add the following lines shown in boldface to the relevant subroutine in the MAIN.FRM code window.

```
Sub MFile_Click (Index As Integer)
...
          Case 2
              If CMDialog1.Filename = "" Then
                  CMDialog1.Action = 1
              End If
              Memory_To_Disk
...
End Sub
```

Preventing loss of data

A good program requires safeguards which prevent unintentional loss of information. By means of a global variable, our program will keep track of whether or not an alteration to the file has been saved. For reasons of convenience, we shall presume that each activation of the input mask leads to modification of the data. The *FileSafe* global variable has the value False if the current version of the file has not yet been saved.

Declare the *FileSafe* global variable (GLOBAL.BAS, Proc: (declarations)) and place the initial value of *FileSafe* in the Form_Load procedure of the Mask form.

```
Global FileSafe As Integer

Sub Form_Load ()
    FileSafe = False
...
End Sub
```

At the start of the program itself, we give the *FileSafe* variable a fixed value. It is logical to assign the value True to this at this stage since there is no reason to save the file at this moment. Add the following command to the Form_Load procedure of the MusicMain form.

```
Sub Form_Load ()
    FileSafe = True
    EmptyRec_Create
End Sub
```

In the Memory_To_Disk global procedure, the safeguard variable gets the value True only after the file has been written to disk using this procedure.

```
Sub Memory_To_Disk ()
...
FileSafe = True
End Sub
```

Up until now, we have only applied a safeguard against data loss in the most straightforward situations. An example of a more complex situation is this: Imagine that the program has been started up and the input mask is closed after data have been entered in a new file. If the *Close* command is given, the data will be lost if there is no control by *FileSafe*.

In order to prevent this, the program performs a test in all situations in which data could be lost. Situations like these occur in the *New, Open* and *Close* menu items. Each time one of these commands is given, the program should execute the local File_Test procedure (in the MusicMain form).

The File_Test procedure first checks if FileSafe=False and if there is at least one filled record. If this is not the case, everything is in order and the program may quit the procedure.

If FileSafe=False, does the program user wish to save the created or altered records? If the answer *Yes* is given via a dialog window, the next step involves a test as to whether or not a filename is known. If there is no filename, the familiar dialog window appears, requesting a name for the file. If the answer *No* is given, the FileSafe flag is assigned the value True and the program user continues by loading another file or creating a new file.

Place the new File_Test procedure in the *(general)* object in the MusicMain form.

```
Sub File_Test ()
    If (FileSafe = False) And (RecPresent > 0)
          Then
        Choice = MsgBox("Do you want to save
            the modified file?", 36)
        If Choice = 6 Then
            If CMDialog1.Filename = "" Then
                CMDialog1.Action = 2
            End If
            Memory_To_Disk
        End If
    End If
    FileSafe = True
End Sub
```

As mentioned, we shall activate this procedure in the *New, Open* and *Close* menu items. With a new file, we must also ensure that there is no filename in memory (e.g. the name of the previous file). In this case, we shall assign an empty string to the *Filename* property of CMDialog1. In addition, the newly allocated initial values of *RecPresent* and *CurRec* should be displayed in the status line (via the StatusLine_Modify procedure). Open the MFile_Click subroutine code in MAIN.FRM and add the lines shown in boldface.

```
Sub MFile_Click (Index As Integer)
On Error GoTo MisCanc
    Select Case Index
        Case 0
            File_Test
            CMDialog1.Filename = ""
            RecPresent = 1
            CurRec = 1
            MusicRec(1) = EmptyRec
            StatusLine_Modify
            Mask.Show 1
        Case 1
            File_Test
            CMDialog1.Action = 1
            Disk_To_Memory
...
        Case 7
            File_Test
            End
...
End Sub
```

6.5 Operating the menus via the program

The contents of the menus should correspond to the current situation in the program:

■ After opening a file containing at least one record, all commands should be available which pertain to an opened file (save, print etc.).
■ In the case of a new file, some menu items should remain inaccessible until the file contains at least one record.

The Menu_Operate global procedure regulates the availability of various menu items.

The Menu_Operate global procedure

The contents of the menus depend on the *RecPresent* global variable and on the *Checked* property of the *List* menu option in the *View* menu.

If the file contains at least one record, the following menu items should be available:

- *Save, Save As* and *Print* in the *File* menu;
- the *Edit* menu;
- *List* in the *View* menu.

Under other circumstances, these commands should be inaccessible. In addition, the *Checked* property of the *List* option should be switched off (the tick mark disappears). The List control disappears from the Music-Main form.

Create the new Menu_Operate procedure in GLO-BAL.BAS (*View, New Procedure*).

```
Sub Menu_Operate ()
    If RecPresent > 0 Then
        MusicMain.MFile(2).Enabled = True
        MusicMain.MFile(3).Enabled = True
        MusicMain.MFile(5).Enabled = True
        MusicMain.EditMenu.Enabled = True
        MusicMain.MView(1).Enabled = True
    Else
        MusicMain.MFile(2).Enabled = False
        MusicMain.MFile(3).Enabled = False
        MusicMain.MFile(5).Enabled = False
        MusicMain.EditMenu.Enabled = False
        MusicMain.MView(1).Enabled = False
        MusicMain.MView(1).Checked = False
        MusicMain.Overview.Visible = False
    End If
```

Depending on the value of the *Checked* property of the *List* menu item, the four options *Selection, Font, Point size* and *Background colour* should be simultaneously available or inaccessible.

```
If MusicMain.MView(1).Checked = True Then
    MusicMain.MView(3).Enabled = True
    MusicMain.MView(4).Enabled = True
    MusicMain.MView(5).Enabled = True
    MusicMain.MView(6).Enabled = True
Else
    MusicMain.MView(3).Enabled = False
    MusicMain.MView(4).Enabled = False
    MusicMain.MView(5).Enabled = False
    MusicMain.MView(6).Enabled = False
End If
End Sub
```

The Menu_Operate procedure is only activated when
the Mask form is left via the *Cancel* or *Close* buttons.
After all, data are only added or modified in the input
mask. Place the command to activate the Menu_Ope-
rate procedure in the procedures dealing with *Close*
and *Cancel* in the Mask form.

```
Sub MaskBClose_Click ()
...
    StatusLine_Modify
    Menu_Operate
    MousePointer = 0
End Sub

Sub MaskBCancel_Click ()
...
    StatusLine_Modify
    Menu_Operate
    Unload Mask
    MousePointer = 0
End Sub
```

In three menu procedures, the Menu_Operate procedure should be activated by means of three commands. Add the lines shown below in boldface to the
appropriate subroutines in the MAIN.FRM code window:

1 View, List

```
Sub MView_Click (Index As Integer)
...
    Case 1
        If MView(1).Checked = False Then
            MView(1).Checked = True
            Overview.Visible = True
        Else
            MView(1).Checked = False
            Overview.Visible = False
        End If
        Menu_Operate
...
End Select
...
End Sub
```

2 File, New

With the *New* command (*Case 0*), the total menu structure should be made identical to that at the beginning of the program. Because the program in the Menu_Operate procedure tests the status of the program by means of the *RecPresent>0* condition, *RecPresent* should be assigned the value 0 in advance.

3 File, Open

With the *Open* command *(Case 1)*, the accessibility of the menu items only needs to be adjusted if the file contains at least one record.

```
Sub MFile_Click (Index As Integer)
...
        Case 0
            File_Test
            RecPresent = 0
            Menu_Operate
            CMDialog1.Filename = ""
...
```

```
                    Case 1
                        File_Test
                        CMDialog1.Action = 1
                        Disk_To_Memory
                        Menu_Operate
            ...
            End Select
            ...
            End Sub
```

6.6   Printing data

When printing a music catalogue file, we shall confine ourselves to printing complete lists. To regulate this we shall use the Common Dialog box control which we have also used elsewhere. Because we do not wish to make all the possibilities available, we shall suppress various elements; this is done by means of the *Flags* variable which is the sum of three separate flags.

Value	Description
&H00100000&	(PD_HIDEPRINTTOFILE) The *Print To File* check box is not shown.
&H00000008&	(PD_NOPAGENUMS) Suppresses the *Pages* option button with the corresponding specification fields.
&H00000004&	(PD_NOSELECTION) Suppresses the *Selection* options button.

The combination of these flags is represented by the sum of the values mentioned: the hexadecimal number &H0010000C&. The Print version of the standard dialog window is activated by the property *Action=5*. Then comes the activation of the Print_Records local procedure.

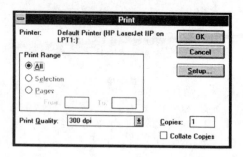

```
Sub MFile_Click (Index As Integer)
...
        Case 5
                CMDialog1.Flags = &H10000C&
                CMDialog1.Action = 5
                Print_Records
...
End Sub
```

We shall place the Print_Records procedure locally in the MusicMain form. The program uses the local dimensioned variable, *PageNumber*, in order to number the pages in the file consecutively.

```
Sub Print_Records ()
MousePointer = 11
Dim PageNumber As Integer
```

The outer loop has the *NumCopies* variable (number of copies) which receives its value from the *Copies* property. In the next command, the screen font which has been specified for the list is adopted as font for the printer. For this we use the TrueType Arial font as default value since we know that this font is available for both the screen and the printer. We have deliberately set the point size to 12 in order to prevent layout problems during the actual printing although we could have made it the same as the overview size by specifying Printer.FontSize = Overview.FontSize. Before the actual print job begins, the page counter (*PageNumber*) is assigned the value 1.

```
For NumCopies = 1 To CMDialog1.Copies
    Printer.FontName = Overview.FontName
    Printer.FontSize = 12
    PageNumber = 1
```

The second loop deals with the records from the file, from 1 up to and including RecPresent.

```
For RecNr = 1 To RecPresent
```

The first command examines whether or not it is time to print the page heading. Because 52 records plus the page heading fit onto a page, the text has to be printed in front of the 1st record, the 53rd record, the 105th record etc. In other words, if RecNr divided by 52 produces a remainder of 1, the program should print the heading.

The *Mod* command calculates the remainder of a division. In our program, we shall divide RecNr by the value shown behind *Mod* (52). If RecNr is a multiple of 52, the remainder will be 0, otherwise it will vary from 1 to 51.

```
If RecNr Mod 52 = 1 Then
```

We shall use the *Print* method for output to the printer. This method sends a text to an object - in this case the printer - along with the specified font and point size. The command *Printer.Print* without further specification produces a blank line. If the text has to be printed at a certain position on the line, that can be done by means of the *Tab()* function.

The position of the text on the paper depends on the selected font. This means that the tab positions for each different font have to be calculated each time. For this reason, we shall use a fixed font (Arial) and a fixed point size (12) in our program. All tabulator values in the listing are valid for these settings.

If different data are printed on one line, the individual print commands have to be concluded with a semi-colon. Without a semi-colon, the subsequent text automatically appears on a new line.

When displaying the name of the file, we use the *Filetitle* property which only shows the name of the file itself and not the accompanying path.

The page heading begins with two blank lines at the top of the page. After the first heading (from *Music Catalogue V1.00* to *PageNumber*), there is another blank line. This means that the page heading will occupy a total of six lines.

```
Printer.Print
Printer.Print
Printer.Print Tab(6);
    "Music Catalogue V1.00";
Printer.Print Tab(40);
    CMDialog1.Filetitle;
Printer.Print Tab(54);
    RecPresent;
Printer.Print Tab(59);
    "records";
Printer.Print Tab(73);
    Format$(Now, "dd.mm.yy");
Printer.Print Tab(86); "Page";
Printer.Print Tab(92);
    PageNumber
Printer.Print
Printer.Print Tab(6); "ARTIST";
Printer.Print Tab(40); "TITLE";
Printer.Print Tab(73); "TYPE";
Printer.Print Tab(81); "#";
Printer.Print Tab(86); "GENRE"
Printer.Print
End If
```

One record is printed on one line (with the exception of the field for notes). Some fields (Artist, Title) are shortened to 25 characters by means of the *Left$()* function, otherwise there is not enough room on one line for all the fields. With the Type data field, there is the problem that this only contains an index which refers to a string. The print procedure must generate the relevant string referring to the sound device in question by means of the Select-Case structure.

```
            Printer.Print Tab(6);
↺               Left$(MusicRec(RecNr).Artist,
↺                  25);
            Printer.Print Tab(40);
↺               Left$(MusicRec(RecNr).Title,
↺                  25);
            Select Case MusicRec(RecNr).Type
               Case 0
                  Printer.Print Tab(73);
↺                  "CD";
               Case 1
                  Printer.Print Tab(73);
↺                  "LP";
               Case 2
                  Printer.Print Tab(73);
↺                  "MC";
               Case 3
                  Printer.Print Tab(73);
↺                  "DAT";
            End Select
            Printer.Print Tab(81); Left$(Music-
↺               Rec(RecNr).Quantity, 2);
            Printer.Print Tab(86); Left$(Music-
↺               Rec(RecNr).Genre, 12);
```

When the sheet is full, the printer has to move on to a new sheet of paper. We use the *Mod* command to find out if the 52nd, the 104th, the 156th etc. record has been printed. Each time the number of records is divisible by 52 (remainder 0), the command activates the *New Page* method. The *PageNumber* variable should then be increased by 1.

```
        If RecNr Mod 52 = 0 Then
            Printer.NewPage
            PageNumber = PageNumber + 1
        End If
    Next RecNr
```

When all records have been printed, there are two possible situations:

1   The last sheet ends exactly at the last record in the file.
2   The last record is positioned somewhere in the middle of the page.

In the second case, we shall instruct the printer to move the paper on to a new page by means of the *New Page* command. We can check whether or not this situation exists by testing if the remainder of the division is equal to 0. If this is the case, the last sheet will be exactly full and the paper need not be moved on.

```
        If RecPresent Mod 52 <> 0 Then
            Printer.NewPage
        End If
```

The *EndDoc* method informs the printer (or the Print Manager print queue) that the document is completed and can be printed.

```
        Printer.EndDoc
    Next NumCopies
MousePointer = 0
End Sub
```

The result of the print procedure is as follows:

Music Catalogue V1.00   SPECTRUM.MUS   75 records   03.07.1994   Page 1

ARTIST	TITLE	TYPE	#	GENRE
AC/DC	Live	CD	2	Hard Rock
AC/DC	High Voltage	CD	1	Hard Rock
AC/DC	Let There Be Rock	CD	1	Hard Rock
AC/DC	Powerage	CD	1	Hard Rock
AC/DC	Live from the Atlantic Studios	CD	1	Hard Rock
Adams, Bryan	Bryan Adams	CD	2	Rock
Adams, Bryan	Waking up the Neighbors	CD	1	Rock
Alice in Chains	Dirt	CD	1	Heavy Metal
Bliss	Loveprayer	CD	1	Pop
Bon Jovi	Slippery When Wet	CD	1	Hard Rock
Bon Jovi	Keep the Faith	CD	1	Hard Rock
Brown,Sam	STOP!	CD	1	Pop
Bush, Kate	Kick Inside	CD	1	Pop
Bush, Kate	Never for Ever	CD	1	Pop
Bush, Kate	Hounds of Love	CD	1	Pop
Bush, Kate	The Sensual World	CD	1	Pop
Bush, Kate	The Red Shoes	CD	1	Pop
Chapman, Tracey	Tracey Chapman	CD	1	FeelThink
Carmel	Set Me Free	CD	1	Jazz
Carmel	The Drum Is Everything	CD	1	Jazz
Carmel	The Falling	CD	1	Jazz
Carpenter, John	They Live	CD	1	Soundtrack
Clapton, Eric	The Cream of Eric Clapton	CD	1	Blues
Clapton, Eric	Journeyman	CD	1	Blues
Collins, Phil	face Value	CD	1	Pop
Coverdale/Page	Coverdale-Page	CD	1	Hard Rock
Cross, The	MAD:BAD	LP	1	Hard Rock
Deepest Purple	The Very Best of Deep Purple	CD	1	Hard Rock
Dire Straits	Brothers in Arms	DAT	1	Rock
Dire Straits	On Every Street	CD	1	Rock
Dubrovniks, The	Audio Sonic Love Affair	CD	1	Hard Rock
Dulfer, Candy	SAXuality	MC	1	Funk
Dulfer, Candy	Sax-a-go-go	LP	1	Funk
Extreme	III Sides To Every Story	CD	1	Hard Rock
Ferry, Bryan	The Ultimate Collection	MC	1	Pop
Gabriel, Peter	Plays Live	CD	2	Rock
Gabriel, Peter	Birdy	CD	1	Soundtrack
Gabriel, Peter	Passion	CD	1	Soundtrack
Gabriel, Peter	Shaking The Tree	CD	1	Rock
Gabriel, Peter	US	CD	1	Rock
Genesis	We Can't Dance	CD	1	Pop
Gothard	Gothard	MC	1	Hard Rock
Guns N' Roses	Appetite for Destruction	CD	1	Heavy Metal
Havenzangers	Rotterdam	LP	1	Dutch senti-mental

Music Catalogue V1.00   SPECTRUM.MUS   75 records   03.07.1994   Page 2

ARTIST	TITLE	TYPE	#	GENRE
Hooker - King	I'll play the Blues for you	MC	1	Blues
Hooker, John Lee	The John Lee Hooker Collection	LP	1	Blues
Hooker, John Lee	Live At Sugar Hill 1 & 2	CD	1	Blues
Hooker, John Lee	Cold Chills	MC	1	Blues
Hooker, John Lee	Don't You Remember Me	CD	1	Blues
Hooker, John Lee	Alone	CD	2	Blues
Hooker, John Lee	The Cream	MC	2	Blues
Hooker, John Lee	The Healer	CD	1	Blues
Hooker, John Lee	Mr. Lucky	MC	1	Blues
Hooker, John Lee	Boom Boom	CD	1	Blues
Hornsby, Bruce	Scenes from the Southside	MC	1	Pop
Isaak, Chris	Wicked Game	CD	1	Pop
Jackson, Joe	Laughter & Lust	MC	1	Pop
Jackson, Joe	Live 1980/86	CD	2	Pop
Jeffreys, Garland	Don't call me Buckwheat	MC	1	Reggae
Jethro Tull	Original Masters	LP	1	Rock
Jethro Tull	Crest of a Knave	LP	1	Rock
Jethro Tull	Rock Island	MC	1	Rock
Kansas	The Best of Kansas	LP	1	Rock
Led Zeppelin	Remasters	CD	2	Hard Rock
Living Colors	Time's up	LP	1	Heavy Metal
Mayall, John	The Power of The Blues	LP	1	Blues
Mayall, John	A Sense of Place	MC	1	Blues
Mercury, Freddie	The Album	CD	1	Rock
Queen	A Night At The Opera	CD	1	Hard Rock
Queen	Queen II	LP	1	Hard Rock
Queen	The Game	LP	1	Hard Rock
Queen	News of the World	CD	1	Hard Rock
Queen	Jazz	MC	1	Hard Rock
Queen	A kind of Magic	CD	1	Hard Rock
Queen	Innuendo	CD	1	Hard Rock

6.7   Filling the data list and displaying it on screen

We shall display the contents of the file on screen using the Grid control. A Grid row corresponds to one record and one column corresponds to one of the data fields of the records.

The structure and working of the Grid which we shall apply here are analogous to those in a worksheet in a spreadsheet program. The top row contains the names of the data fields and the cells in the first column contain the corresponding numbers of the records. This row and column should remain fixed in place even when you browse through the records. The numbers of fixed rows and columns are stored in the *FixedRows* and *FixedCols* properties. The fixed rows and columns always have a grey background.

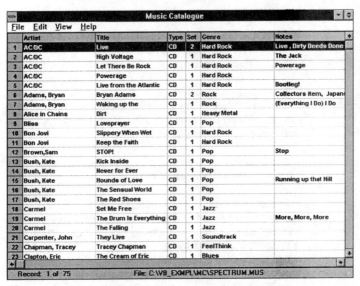

	Artist	Title	Type	Set	Genre		Notes	
1	AC/DC	Live	CD	2	Hard Rock		Live , Dirty Deeds Done	
2	AC/DC	High Voltage	CD	1	Hard Rock		The Jack	
3	AC/DC	Let There Be Rock	CD	1	Hard Rock		Powerage	
4	AC/DC	Powerage	CD	1	Hard Rock			
5	AC/DC	Live from the Atlantic	CD	1	Hard Rock		Bootleg!	
6	Adams, Bryan	Bryan Adams	CD	2	Rock		Collectors item, Japan	
7	Adams, Bryan	Waking up the	CD	1	Rock		(Everything I Do) I Do	
8	Alice in Chains	Dirt	CD	1	Heavy Metal			
9	Bliss	Loveprayer	CD	1	Pop			
10	Bon Jovi	Slippery When Wet	CD	1	Hard Rock			
11	Bon Jovi	Keep the Faith	CD	1	Hard Rock			
12	Brown,Sam	STOP!	CD	1	Pop		Stop	
13	Bush, Kate	Kick Inside	CD	1	Pop			
14	Bush, Kate	Never for Ever	CD	1	Pop			
15	Bush, Kate	Hounds of Love	CD	1	Pop		Running up that Hill	
16	Bush, Kate	The Sensual World	CD	1	Pop			
17	Bush, Kate	The Red Shoes	CD	1	Pop			
18	Carmel	Set Me Free	CD	1	Jazz			
19	Carmel	The Drum Is Everything	CD	1	Jazz		More, More, More	
20	Carmel	The Falling	CD	1	Jazz			
21	Carpenter, John	They Live	CD	1	Soundtrack			
22	Chapman, Tracey	Tracey Chapman	CD	1	FeelThink			
23	Clapton, Eric	The Cream of Eric	CD	1	Blues			

Record: 1 of 75   File: C:\VB_EXMPL\MC\SPECTRUM.MUS

The part of the grid containing the data consists of free rows and columns. The number of columns (fixed plus free) is stored in the *Cols* variable. In our program, this number is 7. The total number of rows depends on the number of records in the file: *Rows=RecPresent+1* (due to the fixed row with the column titles).

Because the Fill_Overview procedure is global, we shall place it in GLOBAL.BAS.

```
Sub Fill_Overview ()
MousePointer = 11
        MusicMain.Overview.Cols = 7
        MusicMain.Overview.Rows = RecPresent + 1
```

The first fixed column has the column number 0 (*Col=0*). Positioning the contents of a field in the cells of the fixed columns is done by means of the *Fixed-Alignment(column number)* property. The most important valid values are:

Value   Effect

0   Left alignment (default setting)
1   Right alignment
2   Centred

The column width is specified by means of the *Col-Width(column number)* property. Visual Basic uses the twip as the unit of measurement here.

```
        MusicMain.Overview.FixedAlignment(0) = 2
        MusicMain.Overview.ColWidth(0) = 400
```

We can address a specific cell in the grid as the intersection of a row and column. For this, the *Row* and *Col* properties are given the values of this intersection. On the fixed row used for the column titles (*Row=0*), we shall define the column width for the cell containing the first title (*Col=1*). Here we specify *ColWidth(0)=2000* and *Text="Artist"*.

```
        MusicMain.Overview.Row = 0
        MusicMain.Overview.Col = 1
        MusicMain.Overview.ColWidth(0) = 2000
        MusicMain.Overview.Text = "Artist"
```

As long as we are on the first row, we do not need to give *Row* a new value. Adopt the values shown below for columns 2 to 6 on this row:

```
MusicMain.Overview.Col = 2
MusicMain.Overview.ColWidth(2) = 2000
MusicMain.Overview.Text = "Title"
MusicMain.Overview.Col = 3
MusicMain.Overview.ColWidth(3) = 500
MusicMain.Overview.Text = "Type"
MusicMain.Overview.Col = 4
MusicMain.Overview.ColAlignment(4) = 2
MusicMain.Overview.ColWidth(4) = 400
MusicMain.Overview.Text = "Set"
MusicMain.Overview.Col = 5
MusicMain.Overview.ColWidth(5) = 2000
MusicMain.Overview.Text = "Genre"
MusicMain.Overview.Col = 6
MusicMain.Overview.ColWidth(6) = 5000
MusicMain.Overview.Text = "Notes"
```

The counter loop with the record number (*RecNr*) as the counter writes the contents of the data fields in the grid.

```
For RecNr = 1 To RecPresent
```

In the fixed column 0, we shall place the record number of the currently active record.

```
MusicMain.Overview.Col = 0
MusicMain.Overview.Row = RecNr
MusicMain.Overview.Text = RecNr
```

Using the *Clip* property, we can fill various fields simultaneously using only one command. A condition of this is that the range to be filled is marked in advance. In our program, the block to be marked always consists of one empty row in which we write the complete contents of a record except for the Type field (the cell for this field is left empty for the moment).

The block to be selected is defined by four properties. For the first block: *SelStartCol=1*, *SelStartRow=RecNr*, *SelEndCol=6* and *SelEndRow=RecNr*.

The contents of the various fields which are distributed across the cells using the *Clip* property have to be separated from one another by means of the Tab key ANSI code (9). We shall apply this value in the output string as the separator to the following cell. We use the *Chr$()* function for this.

```
         MusicMain.Overview.SelStartCol = 1
         MusicMain.Overview.SelStartRow = RecNr
         MusicMain.Overview.SelEndCol = 6
         MusicMain.Overview.SelEndRow = RecNr
         MusicMain.Overview.Clip
↳            = MusicRec(RecNr).Artist + Chr$(9)
↳            + MusicRec(RecNr).Title + Chr$(9)
↳            + "" + Chr$(9)
↳            + MusicRec(RecNr).Quantity + Chr$(9)
↳            + MusicRec(RecNr).Genre + Chr$(9)
↳            + MusicRec(RecNr).Notes
```

In the *Clip* property, we have applied an empty string to the third cell position because the data field only contains an index. We shall use the Select-Case structure to apply the relevant string to the *Text* property in column 3 of the current record.

```
         MusicMain.Overview.Col = 3
         Select Case MusicRec(RecNr).Type
             Case 0
                 MusicMain.Overview.Text = "CD"
             Case 1
                 MusicMain.Overview.Text = "LP"
             Case 2
                 MusicMain.Overview.Text = "MC"
             Case 3
                 MusicMain.Overview.Text = "DAT"
         End Select
     Next RecNr
```

Finally, the procedure marks the current record. We have already used this kind of command block when filling a row.

```
      MusicMain.Overview.SelStartCol = 1
      MusicMain.Overview.SelStartRow = CurRec
      MusicMain.Overview.SelEndCol = 6
      MusicMain.Overview.SelEndRow = CurRec
MousePointer = 0
End Sub
```

Adjusting the size of the overview to the form

In order to prevent the program jamming during execution due to the size of the form window being unsuitable, any adjustment of the grid size to the modified window size may only occur if there is sufficient space (2000 twip) for at least one record. The adjustment of the form window size is carried out by the Form_Resize event procedure which is activated each time the measurements alter. Create the following routine in MAIN.FRM (*View* menu, *New Procedure*).

```
Sub Form_Resize ()
    If (MusicMain.Height > 2000)
↻           And (MusicMain.Width > 2000) Then
        Overview.Height = MusicMain.ScaleHeight
↻            - StatusLine.Height
        Overview.Width = MusicMain.ScaleWidth
    End If
End Sub
```

Activating the Fill_Overview procedure

The Fill_Overview procedure has to be executed in *four cases*:

■ **Open file (MusicMain form)**

```
Sub MFile_Click (Index As Integer)
...
        Case 1
            File_Test
            CMDialog1.Action = 1
            Disk_To_Memory
            Menu_Operate
    .       Fill_Overview
...
End Sub
```

■ **Display List (MusicMain form)**

```
Sub MView_Click (Index As Integer)
...
    Case 1
        If MView(1).Checked = False Then
            MView(1).Checked = True
            Fill_Overview
            Overview.Visible = True
...
End Sub
```

■ **Close input mask (Mask form)**

```
Sub MaskBClose_Click ()
...
    Fill_Overview
     MousePointer = 0
End Sub
```

■ **Cancel input (Mask form)**

```
Sub MaskBCancel_Click ()
...
    Fill_Overview
    Unload Mask
    MousePointer = 0
End Sub
```

Working with the mouse and the cursor keys in the data list

Clicking on a chosen field in a record should activate the record. In addition, the status line should be adjusted. Add the following lines shown in boldface to the appropriate subroutines in MAIN.FRM.

```
Sub Overview_Click ()
    CurRec = Overview.SelStartRow
    StatusLine_Modify
End Sub
```

A double click should do the same but also opens the input mask with the currently active record so that it can be modified.

```
Sub Overview_DblClick ()
    CurRec = Overview.SelStartRow
    StatusLine_Modify
    Mask.Show 1
End Sub
```

We also wish to be able to move through the records using the Cursor Up and the Cursor Down keys; the status line should be adjusted appropriately. Write the following two procedures for the Overview object in MAIN.FRM.

```
Sub Overview_KeyDown (KeyCode As Integer,
↳       Shift As Integer)
    CurRec = Overview.SelStartRow
    StatusLine_Modify
End Sub
```

```
Sub Overview_KeyUp (KeyCode As Integer,
↳       Shift As Integer)
    CurRec = Overview.SelStartRow
    StatusLine_Modify
End Sub
```

A click on the right-hand mouse button at any position in the list should open the *View* menu as a pop-up menu. The MouseDown procedure takes place when any mouse button is pressed. The default value 1 of the *Button* property of the mouse refers to the left mouse button. *Button=2* refers to the right mouse button. The value of *Button* indicates which mouse button is pressed, which provides the possibility of reacting in a chosen way. The PopupMenu method displays the specified menu (which must contain at least one command) at the current cursor position.

```
Sub Overview_MouseDown (Button As Integer,
↪       Shift As Integer, X As Single,
↪       Y As Single)
    If Button = 2 Then
        PopupMenu ViewMenu
    End If
End Sub
```

Selecting categories from the data list

In the SelectionList form (SELECT.FRM) we have placed a number of check boxes which enable you to specify which columns (data fields) are to be displayed in the overview on the screen.

The operation of the selection is included in the Fill_Overview procedure. The SelectBOK_Click procedure only needs to ensure that the list appears on the screen once more according to the altered specifications. The procedure ends with the command to make the form window invisible. We shall not use the *Unload* command to do this this time because that would lead to the entire form with all data being deleted from memory. The *Hide* method makes the form window invisible but all elements remain available to the program and thus can also be edited.

```
Sub SelectBOK_Click ()
    Fill_Overview
    SelectionList.Hide
End Sub
```

As long as the program is active, the selection window should show the data columns available as the standard selection. This selection should therefore be available at the activation of the MusicMain main form, but only visible when selected via the menu. The *Load* command loads the SelectionList form in working memory. At that moment, all columns are shown: we have chosen the *Value=1* setting (which means selected) for all check boxes. Add the following line in boldface to the Form_Load subroutine in MAIN.FRM.

```
Sub Form_Load ()
    FileSafe = True
    EmptyRec_Create
    Load SelectionList
End Sub
```

We shall add a test to the Fill_Overview procedure which indicates for each data column whether or not the corresponding check box has been activated (value =1). If the value is 1, the specified column width is retained, otherwise the width is set to 1 twip. It then seems as if the display has been discontinued, but all data remain present. Add the following lines shown in boldface to the Fill_Overview procedure in GLOBAL.BAS.

```
Sub Fill_Overview ()
MousePointer = 11
    MusicMain.Overview.Cols = 7
    MusicMain.Overview.Rows = RecPresent + 1
    MusicMain.Overview.FixedAlignment(0) = 2
    MusicMain.Overview.ColWidth(0) = 400
    MusicMain.Overview.Row = 0
    MusicMain.Overview.Col = 1
    If SelectionList.Selection(0) = 1 Then
```

```
        MusicMain.Overview.ColWidth(0) = 2000
    Else
        MusicMain.Overview.ColWidth(1) = 1
    End If
    MusicMain.Overview.Text = "Artist"
    MusicMain.Overview.Col = 2
    If SelectionList.Selection(1) = 1 Then
        MusicMain.Overview.ColWidth(2) = 2000
    Else
        MusicMain.Overview.ColWidth(2) = 1
    End If
    MusicMain.Overview.Text = "Title"
    MusicMain.Overview.Col = 3
    If SelectionList.Selection(2) = 1 Then
        MusicMain.Overview.ColWidth(3) = 400
    Else
        MusicMain.Overview.ColWidth(3) = 1
    End If
    MusicMain.Overview.Text = "Type"
    MusicMain.Overview.Col = 4
    MusicMain.Overview.ColAlignment(4) = 2
    If SelectionList.Selection(3) = 1 Then
    MusicMain.Overview.ColWidth(4) = 400
    Else
        MusicMain.Overview.ColWidth(4) = 1
    End If
    MusicMain.Overview.Text = "Set"
    MusicMain.Overview.Col = 5
    If SelectionList.Selection(4) = 1 Then
        MusicMain.Overview.ColWidth(5) = 2000
    Else
        MusicMain.Overview.ColWidth(5) = 1
    End If
    MusicMain.Overview.Text = "Genre"
    MusicMain.Overview.Col = 6
    MusicMain.Overview.ColWidth(6) = 5000
    MusicMain.Overview.Text = "Notes"
...
End Sub
```

Our version of the Music Catalogue project is now completed. Of course it's up to you if you want to extend or modify the program. Do your best!

Exercises

1   Which dialog windows can be generated by the Common Dialog control?

   _____

   _____

2   Calculate the value produced by adding up the following values of the *Flags* property.

   ```
   &H08000&
   &H04000&
   &H00080&
   &H00020&
   ─────────── +
   ```

   _____

3   Calculate the decimal value of the hexadecimal number &H01A2F&.

   _____

4   How do you define an own particular data type and what are the advantages of this when programming?

   _____

   _____

5   Which functions remove superfluous spaces at the beginning and end of a string?

   _____

6   What is the difference between the *MsgBox* command and the *MsgBox()* function?

   _____

   _____

7   How does the sorting procedure in the Music Catalogue project check if the records are in the proper order of sequence?

   _____

   _____

8 Why do we use the *Input$()* to load a string and the *Input* command to load integers?

_____

_____

9 Which method leads to the printer moving on to a new page and how do we inform the printer that the print output is completed?

_____

Answers

1 Which dialog windows can be generated by the Common Dialog control?

The Open, Save As, Color, Font, Print dialog windows (and also the activation of the WIN-HELP.EXE Windows program).

2 Calculate the value produced by adding up the following values of the *Flags* property.

```
&H08000&
&H04000&
&H00080&
&H00020&
——————— +
&H0C0A0&
```

3 Calculate the decimal value of the hexadecimal number &H01A2F&.

Split the hexadecimal number and calculate the position values separately:

```
&H0000F& = 15 *    1 =    15
&H00020& =  2 *   16 =    32
&H00A00& = 10 *  256 =  2560
&H01000& =  1 * 4098 =  4098
                     ——————— +
                        6705
```

4   How do you define an own particular data type and what are the advantages of this when programming?

By means of the keyword *Type* we can create a new data type from a number of variables. New variables can be declared by means of this data type. This makes it possible to assign a different value to diverse variables by means of one specification.

5   Which functions remove superfluous spaces at the beginning and end of a string?

The functions *LTrim$()*, *RTrim$()* and *Trim$()*.

6   What is the difference between the *MsgBox* command and the *MsgBox()* function?

The *MsgBox()* function produces a function value (the code of the command button which is pressed) which is used in the program; the *MsgBox* command generates a message box.

7   How does the sorting procedure in the Music Catalogue project check if the records are in the proper order of sequence?

The value of the *SortFlag* variable indicates whether or not records have been switched in the previous loop.

8   Why do we use the *Input$()* to load a string and the *Input* command to load integers?

Using the *Input$()* function, it is possible to specify the number of characters that are to be loaded. The *Input* command works with data types with a fixed length, such as integers.

9   Which method leads to the printer moving on to a new page and how do we inform the printer that the print output is completed?

The *NewPage* method leads to the output being reproduced on a new page. The *EndDoc* method registers the end of the document.

7   The ADDRESS project

In the two previous chapters you have become familiar with the management of data files. In this chapter, we shall create a small address management program, based on the Data control. This control makes it possible to browse through an *existing* data file. The Data control works analogous to the browse functions of the Mask form in the Music Catalogue project. It is in fact obvious that the ready-made Data control will provide more facilities and is easier to operate than our example: all procedures which we wrote with blood, sweat and tears in the previous chapter are standardly available in a Data control. We defined our own data structure for the Music Catalogue; the Data control can address data which are stored in an existing database and also modify them. It is however, not possible in Visual Basic to use the Data control to create a new data file.

By means of our example program, you will gain insight into the workings of a database and the way in which you can make use of it. It is not easy to quickly design an efficient structure for a database and to create direct retrieval routines for the data. This requires not only programming experience to develop a user-oriented database program, insight into the principles of a relational database is also necessary. In addition, the possibilities provided by the Data control in the standard version are so limited that we can only demonstrate the first principles of complex database application. If you wish to develop serious database applications, we advise you to acquire the Professional Version.

Because the Data control is based on the Microsoft Access package, we recommend you to consult the manual dealing with that package and other relevant literature if you wish to know more about relational data management.

7.1 ADDRESS, the project description

As mentioned, the Address project is to manage address records in an existing database. The project will provide all the elementary functions: the possibility to modify, add and delete records, and to search for specific records according to certain criteria. The Data control provides the necessary functions for browsing through each record. We shall create a separate form for the search function. The other functions will all be part of the Address form.

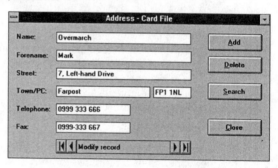

7.2 ADDRESS, creating the work area

Place the following controls in the new form, Form1:

- four Command buttons
- seven Text boxes
- one Data control
- six Label boxes.

The Search form (Form2) is to consist of two command buttons, one Text box and one Label box.

Save the project under the name ADDRESS.MAK in the \VB\VB_EXMPL directory; allocate the name AD-DRESS.FRM to the Form1 form file and the name SEARCH.FRM to Form2.

7.3 ADDRESS, creating the database

Prior to assigning the required properties to the controls, we shall first create the database containing the addresses. As mentioned, it is not possible to create a new database during the execution of the program in the standard version of Visual Basic: the Data control only provides access to existing databases. The Data Manager program which is part of the Visual Basic package can create a database file by means of Microsoft Access (Version 1.0 or 1.1), FoxPro, Paradox or dBASE.

Start the data management program by giving the *Data Manager* command from the *Window* menu (Alt-W, A).

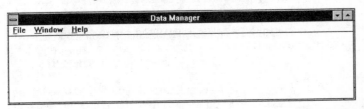

For our project, we shall create a database by means
of version 1.1 of Microsoft Access. Give the command
New Database from the *File* menu (Alt-F, N) and then
choose *Access 1.1* from the submenu (C).

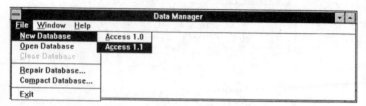

In the subsequent dialog window, create the database
with the name ADDRESS.MDB in the VB\VB_
EXMPL\ADDRESS directory. Confirmation of the input
opens a design window for the tables which are to belong to the database.

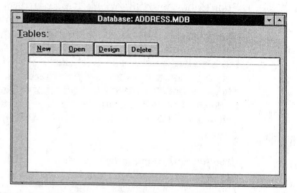

A database can consist of various data files. However,
we only need one data file for our Address project. We
shall give the name AddressTab to this data file.

Click on the *New* button and type the name *Address-
Tab* in the dialog window. When you click on *OK*, a dialog window opens in which you can define the data
fields.

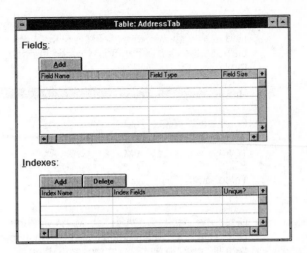

You define the data fields of the records in the upper part of the window. You can specify the fields which are to be used to index the file in the lower part. We shall not deal with this topic here since it falls outside the scope of this book.

The *Add* button opens the *Add Field* dialog window. Enter the Name, Type and Size (length in characters) of the field. There is an options list of valid field types at *Field Type*. We are already familiar with the types Integer, Text and Boolean (True or False). We shall only use the Text type for our Address project.

The first field in the Address file records is assigned the name *Name*, the type is *Text* and the length is *30*.

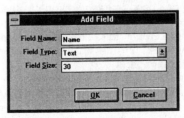

Confirm the input by clicking on *OK*. The Name data field is now shown in the field list of the AddressTab table. Use the *Add* button again to add the data below to the list:

Name	Type	Size
Forename	Text	15
Street	Text	30
Town	Text	30
PC	Text	8
Telephone	Text	20
Fax	Text	20

Close the *Table: AddressTab* window (*Window* menu, *Database:*). In the previous project we wrote a new data file with an empty first record. In this present case, the first record must be filled otherwise the database cannot be edited.

Use the *Open* button to open the current database. In principle, this window contains the same functions as the Mask Form in the Music Catalogue project. There is a difference in that you can only add a record by clicking on the *Add* button. Add any random record by clicking on *Add* and click on *Add* once more to save the record. In contrast to the Mask form, the Data Manager writes the data immediately to the data file on disk for safety reasons. Quit the Field window by clicking on *Close* in the Control menu (click on the small bar in the upper left-hand corner of the window). Quit the Data Manager by pressing Alt-F, X.

Notes: If a database is damaged due to the computer jamming or due to a power failure, you can attempt to repair the damage by selecting *Repair Database* from the *File* (Alt-F, R) menu of the Data Manager.

You can save space on the disk by saving the file in compressed form. The *Compact Database* command from the *File* menu (Alt-F, M) removes empty spaces from the data file.

7.4   ADDRESS, defining the properties

The Address form (ADDRESS.FRM)

Assign the properties shown below to Form1.

Form1 Form
BackColor	= &H00C0C0C0&
BorderStyle	= 1 - Fixed Single
Caption	= Address - Card File
Height	= 4040
Icon	= C:\VB\ICONS\OFFICE\ CRDFILE11.ICO
Left	= 1100
MaxButton	= False
Name	= AddressForm
Top	= 1450
Width	= 7350

Note: The Data control is only usable if the DOS program SHARE.EXE is loaded. Check if the
startup program AUTOEXEC.BAT contains a
command which activates the Share program,
e.g. SHARE.EXE /L:500. If necessary, add this
command.

The Data1 control must be informed which database it
has to work with. The name of this database is registered in the *DatabaseName* property. Double click on
the *DatabaseName* property. Specify in the subsequent dialog box the name of the data file, C:\VB\VB_
EXMPL\ADDRESS\ADDRESS.MDB.

The *RecordSource* property contains the name of the
table with the records to be edited. Mark this property
and open the input box list by clicking on the arrow
pointing downwards. The names of all available databases appear. In our case, this is only the AddressTab
database. Adopt this name into the *RecordSource*
property by clicking on it.

Assign the following properties to the Data1 control:

Data1 Data
BackColor	= &H00C0C0C0&
DatabaseName	= C:\VB\VB_EXMPL\ADDRESS\ ADDRESS.MDB
Height	= 375
Left	= 1320
Top	= 3120
Width	= 3730

The data in the database are edited via a dynamic link between the data fields of the current record and the accompanying controls in the work window. This can only be done with *bound controls*. In the standard version of the program, these are the Check box, the Image box, the Label box, the Picture box and the Text box. These controls are linked by Data to the data fields in the database.

The dynamic link between the first field (Name) and the first text box (Text1) is made via the *DataField* property. The *DataSource* property defines the control used for the link to the database.

When assigning the properties, we have to keep in mind the hierarchy in the linking process. With the Data control, the database is first specified and then the table which is selected from it. Accordingly, we first assign the *DataSource* property and then the *DataField* property.

Text1 TextBox
DataField	= Name
DataSource	= Data1
Height	= 300
Left	= 1320
MaxLength	= 30
Name	= AName
TabIndex	= 0
Top	= 240
Width	= 3720

Text2 TextBox
DataField	= Forename
DataSource	= Data1
Height	= 300
Left	= 1320
MaxLength	= 15
Name	= AForename
TabIndex	= 1
Top	= 720
Width	= 3730

Text3 TextBox
DataField	= Street
DataSource	= Data1
Height	= 300
Left	= 1320
MaxLength	= 30
Name	= AStreet
TabIndex	= 2
Top	= 1200
Width	= 3730

Text4 TextBox
DataField	= Town
DataSource	= Data1
Height	= 300
Left	= 1320
MaxLength	= 30
Name	= ATown
TabIndex	= 3
Top	= 1680
Width	= 2600

Text5 TextBox
DataField	= PC
DataSource	= Data1
Height	= 300
Left	= 4000
MaxLength	= 9
Name	= APC
TabIndex	= 4
Top	= 1680
Width	= 1050

Text6 TextBox
DataField   = Telephone
DataSource   = Data1
Height   = 300
Left   = 1320
MaxLength   = 20
Name   = ATelephone
TabIndex   = 5
Top   = 2160
Width   = 2050

Text7 TextBox
DataField   = Fax
DataSource   = Data1
Height   = 300
Left   = 1320
MaxLength   = 20
Name   = AFax
TabIndex   = 6
Top   = 2640
Width   = 2050

Label1 Label
BackColor   = &H00C0C0C0& (light grey)
Caption   = Name:
Height   = 250
Left   = 215
Top   = 275
Width   = 1000

Label2 Label
BackColor   = &H00C0C0C0& (light grey)
Caption   = Forename:
Height   = 250
Left   = 215
Top   = 765
Width   = 1000

Label3 Label
BackColor   = &H00C0C0C0& (light grey)
Caption   = Street:
Height   = 250
Left   = 215
Top   = 1250
Width   = 1000

Label4 Label
BackColor   = &H00C0C0C0& (light grey)
Caption   = Town/PC:
Height   = 250
Left   = 215
Top   = 1730
Width   = 1000

Label5 Label
BackColor   = &H00C0C0C0& (light grey)
Caption   = Telephone:
Height   = 250
Left   = 215
Top   = 2210
Width   = 1000

Label6 Label
BackColor   = &H00C0C0C0& (light grey)
Caption   = Fax:
Height   = 250
Left   = 215
Top   = 2690
Width   = 1000

Command1 CommandButton
Caption   = &Add
Height   = 450
Left   = 5520
Name   = ABAdd
TabIndex   = 7
Top   = 240
Width   = 1500

Command2 CommandButton
Caption   = &Delete
Height   = 450
Left   = 5520
Name   = ABDelete
TabIndex   = 8
Top   = 840
Width   = 1500

Command3 CommandButton
Caption   = &Search
Height   = 450
Left   = 5520
Name   = ABSearch
TabIndex   = 9
Top   = 1560
Width   = 1500

Command4 CommandButton
Caption   = &Close
Height   = 450
Left   = 5520
Name   = ABClose
TabIndex   = 10
Top   = 2520
Width   = 1500

When the program is started up (press F5), the window
should look like this:

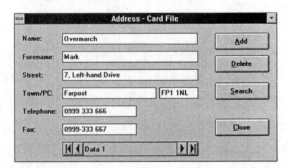

The result shows that the pilot form of the program has access from the Test Box linked control, via the Data1 control, to the test record in the database. Thus, the link between the database on disk and the data in the input fields is there without us having even written one program line! The link has been created by the allocation of appropriate values to the relevant controls.

The Search form (SEARCH.FRM)

Assign the following properties to the Search form:

Form2 Form
BackColor	= &H00C0C0C0& (light grey)
BorderStyle	= 3 - Fixed Double
Caption	= Address search
ControlBox	= False
Height	= 1960
Left	= 2270
MaxButton	= False
MinButton	= False
Name	= SearchFm
Top	= 2500
Width	= 4800

Text1 TextBox
Height	= 300
Left	= 120
MaxLength	= 30
Name	= SearchText
TabIndex	= 0
Text	=
Top	= 360
Width	= 4450

Command1 CommandButton

Caption	= &OK
Height	= 450
Left	= 480
Name	= SearchBOK
TabIndex	= 1
Top	= 960
Width	= 1500

Command2 CommandButton

Cancel	= True
Caption	= &Cancel
Height	= 450
Left	= 2760
Name	= SearchBCanc
TabIndex	= 2
Top	= 960
Width	= 1500

Label1 Label

BackColor	= &H00C0C0C0& (light grey)
Caption	= Name or Forename:
Height	= 250
Left	= 120
Top	= 120
Width	= 1950

7.5   ADDRESS, writing the program code

The Address form (ADDRESS.FRM)

In this example, as previously, we shall first write the closing procedure.

```
Sub ABClose_Click ()
    End
End Sub
```

The Data1 control should contain the text *Modify record* at the beginning of the program because this control automatically creates the link to the first record in the file and displays this record.

```
Sub Form_Load ()
    Data1.Caption = "Modify record"
End Sub
```

The same should take place when the left mouse button is pressed while the mouse pointer is positioned on one of the four browse command buttons.

```
Sub Data1_MouseDown (Button As Integer, Shift
↳        As Integer, X As Single, Y As Single)
    Data1.Caption = "Modify record"
End Sub
```

We need an empty record to be able to include *new records* in the file. The Data1 control gives a constant indication via the *Caption* property of which activity is taking place.

The *RecordSet* property activates a particular record in the opened database. It is as if a door has been opened to the specified record. The combination of *RecordSet* with a method such as *AddNew*, *Move* and *Find* makes it possible to edit a chosen record from the database.

The *AddNew* method creates the required new record. This method generates an empty copy buffer for the current record. Then the first input field is activated by means of the *SetFocus* command.

```
Sub ABAdd._Click ()
    Data1.Caption = "Add new record"
    Data1.RecordSet.AddNew
    AName.SetFocus
End Sub
```

The *Delete* method clears the current record from the database. Before this actually happens, a dialog window should appear in which the program requests confirmation as a safeguard. The answer Yes (code 6) activates the *Delete* method. An orderly deletion should also ensure that after deletion has occurred, another record becomes the currently active record. Because in general there has also been a previous record, we shall apply the *MovePrevious* method for this action. The only exception to this rule will be when the record being deleted is the first record in the file. To check this, the program employs the question BOF=True (Beginning Of File). If so, the record pointer moves to the next record by means of the *MoveNext* method.

```
Sub ABDelete_Click ()
    Answer = MsgBox("Do you really want to
            delete the record?", 20)
    If Answer = 6 Then
        Data1.RecordSet.Delete
        Data1.RecordSet.MovePrevious
        If Data1.RecordSet.BOF = True Then
            Data1.RecordSet.MoveNext
        End If
    End If
    AName.SetFocus
End Sub
```

The *Search* button is to open the SEARCH.FRM form.

```
Sub ABSearch_Click ()
    SearchFm.Show 1
    AName.SetFocus
End Sub
```

The SearchFm form (SEARCH.FRM)

The program looks for a specific record based on the search string which is entered in the SearchText text box. The *OK* command button starts the search procedure.

The *FindFirst* method searches in the database for the first record in which the specified fields correspond to the search string. The search procedure is coded with keywords from the SQL (Structured Query Language). In our example, we use the *Like* operator which compares two strings. The search command consists of six elements in this case:

1 **"Name**
   The data field which is first examined.
2 **Like**
   The comparison operator.
3 **'"**
   An apostrophe as separator in the search string to mark the specified search string.
4 **+ SearchText.Text +**
   The specified search string which is to be compared with the contents of the Name data field.
5 **"*'**
   An extension of the search string which makes it possible to search using an incomplete search string: this works analogous to the wildcards in MS-DOS. The inverted commas conclude the specified search string in the search command. In our example, the search string consists of the value of the *Text* property, and the * wildcard.
6 **Or Forename Like '"+ SearchText.Text + "*'"**
   The *Or* operator means that not only the Name data field is examined but also the Forename field.

```
Sub SearchBOK_Click ()
    AddressForm.Data1.RecordSet.FindFirst "Name
↻       Like '" + SearchText.Text + "*' Or
↻       Forename Like '" + SearchText.Text
↻       + "*'"
    Unload SearchFm
End Sub
```

The *Cancel* button closes the SearchFM form without the search procedure being executed

```
Sub SearchBCanc_Click()
    Unload SearchFm
End Sub
```

Save the program and check that it works properly.

Exercises

1   Which components make up a database and which features are used to declare the basic elements?

    _____

    _____

2   Which properties and controls create the link to a database using Microsoft Access and in which order of sequence must the values be specified?

    _____

    _____

    _____

    _____

Answers

1   Which components make up a database and which features are used to declare the basic elements?

    A database consists of tables. The smallest logical element in a table is a (data) field. The declaration of a field consists of the field name, the field type and the size of the field.

2   Which properties and controls create the link to a database using Microsoft Access and in which order of sequence must the values be specified?

    The link is created via the *DatabaseName* and *RecordSource* properties of the Data control and the

DataField and *DataSource* properties of the linked control (the so-called *bound control*).

First specify the name of the database by entering the *DatabaseName* and then the name of the required table in the database at *RecordSource*. The control in a data window is linked using the *DataSource* property to the Data control. The *DataField* property is used to assign the contents of the specified data field to the appropriate window.

Appendix A
Preparing to work with Visual Basic

System requirements

In order to be able to work smoothly with Visual Basic, the minimum hardware and software requirements are as follows:

Hardware:

■ A compatible personal computer with an Intel processor of the type 80386 or 80486 (SX or DX) and at least 4 Mb working memory.

■ Windows and the standard version of Visual Basic require a total of approximately 20 Mb disk capacity. The actual disk capacity you will need depends on the other packages you want to use.

■ A graphic card which supports at least the VGA standard, although a higher resolution is recommended.

■ A matrix printer is sufficient to be able to print out the program code.

■ Working without a mouse in Visual Basic is absolutely no fun!

Software:

■ MS-DOS 5.0 or higher or OS/2 version 2.1 or higher.

■ Microsoft Windows version 3.1 or higher, or WIN-OS2 which, from version 2.1 onwards, is a part of OS/2.

Installing Visual Basic

Visual Basic is installed on the harddisk by the SETUP.EXE program on diskette 1. The files on the diskettes supplied are compressed. They are decompressed during the installation and subsequently copied to various directories on the harddisk.

Insert the first diskette in the appropriate drive on your computer. In the examples we shall give, we shall refer to 3.5 inch diskettes in drive A:.

If you have not ye started Windows, activate the Setup program by giving the following command behind the DOS prompt:

```
win a:setup
```

If Windows is already started up, activate Setup via the Program Manager. Click on the **File** menu of the Program Manager and select **Run** (this can also be done by pressing Alt-F and then R). A dialog box appears. Type *a:setup* in the text box and confirm the command by pressing Enter or clicking on *OK*.

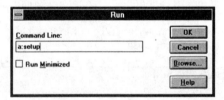

The opening screen welcomes you and indicates that you can discontinue the installation procedure at any chosen moment by choosing the *Cancel Setup* button. Proceed by clicking on *Continue* or by pressing Enter. The subsequent dialog box requests your name. Type it and proceed by clicking on *Continue*. The program suggests installing Visual Basic in the C:\VB directory. If you do not wish to adopt this proposal, delete the letters and type the required path and directory. The program then creates the specified directory, states that it is examining the available disk space and then asks if you want to have a *Complete Installation* or a *Custom Installation*. If you opt for the complete installation, all files and programs will be copied, including the tutorials and the sample files. If you have the Standard Edition of Visual Basic, you will require at least 10 Mb disk capacity for this. If you have the Professional Edition, you will need at least 21 Mb. If you opt for the custom installation, you specify yourself which components you wish to install.

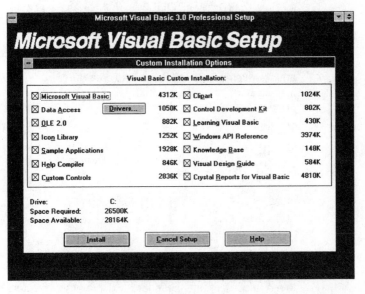

We advise you to implement a complete installation. You will not need the Sample Applications and the Learning Visual Basic program when working with this book, but they do contain many ideas and tips which may be very useful when you get down to making your own programs with Visual Basic. Nevertheless, if you do not want to implement a complete installation now, you can always do so later if necessary.

The Setup program decompresses the files on diskette 1 and copies them to the harddisk. A bar displayed on the screen indicates the progress. After a short while, the program asks you to insert the next diskette in the appropriate drive. Do so and press Enter. When all the diskettes have been copied, a dialog window will state that the installation has been completed. You will also receive a message that the starting-up file AUTO-EXEC.BAT must contain a command line which activates the SHARE.EXE program if you want to make use of operating elements for communal usage, and locking files (DATA and OLE 2.0). In that case, place the line SHARE.EXE /L:500 in AUTOEXEC.BAT. You can close the installation procedure by returning to Windows or by starting the Visual Basic 3.0 program. Switch to Windows and go to the File Manager to examine which directories Setup has created.

The figure shows two levels of the directory tree when a complete installation of the Professional Edition has taken place. In the Standard Edition, the directory structure is much less extensive:

Directory   **Explanation**

VB   Contains the main program VB.EXE, the utility file VB.HLP and other program components.

ICONS   Contains a series of directories with thematically ordered icon files (*.ICO), which you can use in your own applications.

SAMPLES   Contains a series of directories with sample programs.

SETUPKIT   Contains two directories with the Application Setup Wizard and the files which are necessary to create an installation program.

VB.CBT   Contains the instruction program.

The installation program has also copied several files to the \WINDOWS\SYSTEM program. These are files with the extension DLL (Dynamic Link Library) and also files with extra operating elements, with the extension VBX. The function and the application possibilities of these files are dealt with in chapter 7 and Appendix B respectively.

The Visual Basic 3.0 program group

The installation program has created a program group in the Main group, under the name Visual Basic 3.0.

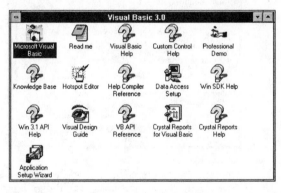

With the Professional Edition, the group contains sixteen icons. With the Standard Edition, there are four.

1 Microsoft Visual Basic program file

In both versions, the Visual Basic icon is displayed in the upper left-hand corner. You can start up the program by double clicking on this icon.

2 The Read me file

The README.TXT text file contains information and alterations which have been made to the program since the manual was printed. You can read this file in the Notepad if you double click on the *Read me* icon. Select the *Print* option from the *File* menu in the Notepad if you wish to obtain the contents of the *Read me* file on paper.

3 Visual Basic Help

In the program group, you can open the list of contents of the Help function by double clicking on the *Visual Basic Help* icon. When in the Visual Basic program itself, you can do the same by selecting the *Contents* option from the *Help* menu (Alt-H, C).

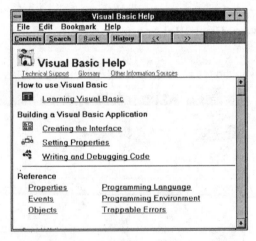

The help pages displayed provide various switch areas (icons and underlined text). At those positions, the mouse pointer changes into a hand with an extended forefinger. The underlining may consist of a normal or a dotted line. The former refers to the topic named; the dotted line indicates that you can gain a definition of the term by clicking on it.

An example: open the help pages of the *Trappable Errors* by clicking anywhere on these words.

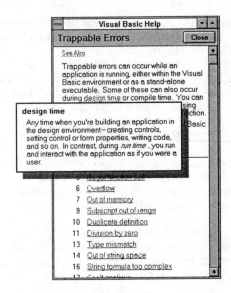

In the explanatory text at the top of the Trappable Errors information, the term *design time* is underlined with a dotted line. If you click on this, a small window will open, providing information concerning that concept. You can close that window once more by clicking anywhere or by pressing Enter.

You can operate the help system by means of the button bar under the menubar of the help window. The *Contents* button produces the list of contents in the help system. If you activate the *Search* button, a dialog window appears enabling you to search for a specific topic or command. Type the relevant word and the program searches for the concept which fits the topic most closely. Then click on *Show Topics* to see what the help program can provide on that subject. The *Search* button works in exactly the same way as the *Search for Help on* option from the *Help* menu in the Program

Manager (Alt-H, S). The *Back* button enables you to move backwards to the pages you summoned previously. The *History* button provides a list of all topics which you examined previously in Visual Basic help. The buttons with the arrows, << and >>, move you respectively to the previous and the next topic in the internal structure of the help system.

4   The Application Setup Wizard

The Application Setup Wizard enables you to create a marketable independent version of an application you have created using Visual Basic. Thus, this utility program is quite different to the Setup installation program used to install Visual Basic itself!

The Application Setup Wizard creates an executable version of your application and also copies the corresponding VBX and DLL files for it in compressed form to the target diskette for your program.

The instruction program

The tutorial on using Visual Basic can be started up in Visual Basic by selecting the option *Learning Microsoft Visual Basic* from the *Help* menu (Alt-H, L).

Start a lesson by clicking on the required icon (or by pressing the underlined letter). The *Instructions* lesson provides information about using the instruction program. Leave the program by selecting the *Exit* button.

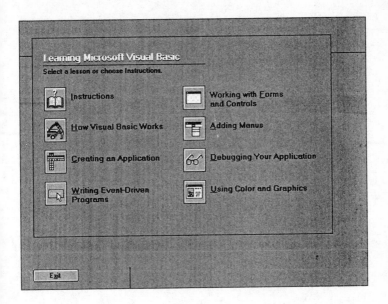

Appendix B
The Visual Basic interface

Those who are not yet acquainted with Visual Basic are advised to read this appendix first in order to become familiar with the most important concepts and windows used in Visual Basic.

With the exception of the toolbar and the toolbox, the other windows will be dealt with in the exercises (projects). If you have already worked with Visual Basic, you will probably have a grasp of most of the information in this appendix.

When you start Visual Basic from the *Visual Basic 3.0* group, the screen will look something like this:

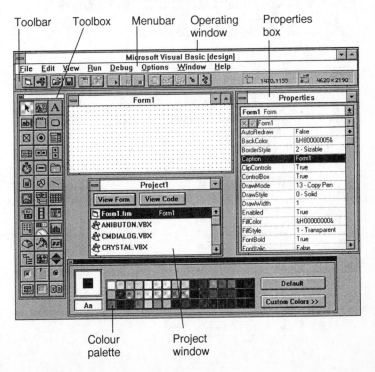

Toolbar   Toolbox   Menubar   Operating window   Properties box

Colour palette   Project window

The Visual Basic work environment consists of various windows. You can open, close and move all these windows just like all other windows under Windows. Excepting the toolbox and the colour palette, you can alter the size of the windows and also reduce them to icons when required.

The design window

The design window is the main window in Visual Basic. All other windows and modes are operated from this window. If you close this window, all other windows are also closed and your session with Visual Basic is brought to an end. The design window contains the menubar and the toolbar.

The menubar

The menubar contains various menus with which you will be familiar from other Windows applications, such as the *File* menu and the *Edit* menu. Click on the *File* menu or press the key combination Alt-F.

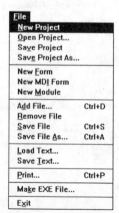

The menu contains several commands with dots behind them. If you activate one of these options, a dialog window appears in which you must enter supplementary information. Only then can the command be implemented. A shortcut key combination is displayed next to some commands. This enables you to give the command easily and quickly by pressing this combination at any required moment in the program. The key combination Ctrl-P for instance, opens the *Print* dialog window for the print options.

The *File* menu also provides commands for opening a project or form, for saving it, for adding files or text to the project, for removing them, for printing (part of) the project or for converting a project to an executable EXE program.

A *Form* is a standardized way of exchanging information. In Visual Basic a form resembles an operating element on the screen, such as a button (for input) or a dialog window (for input and/or output).

In addition to commands for removing, copying or inserting parts of a program or project, the *Edit* menu also contains commands for searching for or replacing program code. There are also commands to place operating elements in the foreground, in the background or for aligning them according to the grid.

The commands in the *View* menu activate the codes window of a Form (function key F7) and manage the routines and functions procedures. The *Toolbar* option enables you to display or hide the toolbar.

The *Run* menu enables you to start and end your program.

The options for testing, monitoring and debugging a program are contained in the *Debug* menu.

The Visual Basic work environment (colour settings, grids etc.) for the currently active project (start up form, command line argument etc.) are specified by means of the options in the *Options* menu.

The *Window* menu enables you to open windows which are not currently visible, and to activate the Visual Basic Data Manager.

The Help function, the tutorial and the orientation program are started up via the *Help* menu.

The toolbar

The toolbar contains fourteen icons which can be activated by clicking with the mouse. There are no shortcut keys for these, although all these icons have their equivalents in the menus, which can be activated using the keyboard. As already mentioned, the toolbar can be displayed or hidden by clicking on the *Toolbar* option in the *View* menu.

  1 2   3   4   5   6   7 8   9   10 11 12 13 14

1   NEW FORM (Alt+F,F)
       Creates a new form and adds it to the current project.
2   NEW MODULE (Alt+F,M)
       Creates a new module and adds it to the current project.
3   OPEN PROJECT (Alt+F,O)
       Closes the current project and opens an existing project.
4   SAVE PROJECT (Ctrl+S or Alt+F,S)
       Saves the current project along with the forms and modules which belong to it.
5   MENU DESIGN WINDOW (Ctrl+M or Alt+W,M)
       Opens the design window for a menu.
6   PROPERTIES WINDOW (F4 or Alt+W,O)
       Opens the properties window.

7   RUN (F5 or Alt+R,S)
    Runs the application during the design mode.
8   BREAK (Ctrl+Break)
    Interrupts the execution of a program (only availa-
    ble during the execution of programs).
9   END (Alt+R,E)
    Stops the execution of a program and returns to
    the design mode.
10 BREAKPOINT (F9 or Alt+D,T)
    On/off switch (toggle) to insert or remove a break-
    point on the current line (only available during the
    execution of programs).
11 INSTANT WATCH (Shift+F9 or Alt+D,I)
    Displays a dialog window with the current value of
    a variable, feature or other expression (only availa-
    ble in the break mode).
12 CALLS (Ctrl+L or Alt+D,C)
    Displays a list of the active procedure calls (only
    available in the break mode).
13 SINGLE STEP (F8 or Alt+D,S)
    Carries out the code, line by line in the code win-
    dow.
14 PROCEDURE STEP (Shift+F8 or Alt+D,P)
    Carries out the code for each function and proce-
    dure in the code window.

At the right of the toolbar, there are two boxes with
number indications.

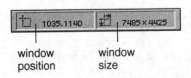

window   window
position   size

The left box indicates the *position* of a selected form or
operating element in relation to the upper left-hand corner of the screen. The distances are measured in units
of *twip* which is specific to Visual Basic. This unit is independent of the screen in use and the printer installed. Usage of twip guarantees that the forms and
controls (operating elements) of your applications al-

ways have the same exact mutual positions, regardless of the screen resolution. This also applies to reproduction on paper. An inch is equal to 1440 twip, a centimetre is roughly 567 twip.

The right box indicates the *size* of a form or a marked operating element. These measurements are also shown in twips.

The form window

The form windows are where you make the windows and dialog windows for use in your programs; they are the 'information hatches'. In addition to normal forms there are also *multiple document interfaces* (MDIs). An MDI form serves as a background and as an environment window for one or more forms at a lower level (*child forms*). An MDI form can only contain menus, icon fields and controls defined by the user. MDI forms are useful when writing applications in which it is possible to have several working windows open simultaneously. Examples of applications which make use of this principle are the Word for Windows word processor and the Excel spreadsheet program.

The toolbox

The toolbox in the standard version of Visual Basic contains the controls (operating elements) which can be used in a form or which can be used to draw controls. There are 22 of these, plus the pointer. The toolbox in the Professional Edition of Visual Basic contains 38 controls, excluding the pointer. The extra buttons in the Professional Edition are positioned in the lower section of the toolbox. Refer to page 14 for an illustration of the Professional Edition toolbox.

You can extend the standard collection of tools yourself by adding extra controls. These controls can be purchased by third-party suppliers or as shareware in shops or on bulletin boards. A file containing additional controls has the extension VBX (Visual Basic eXtra). When Visual Basic is installed, a number of VBX files are copied to the Windows system directory (\WINDOWS\SYSTEM). The number of files copied depends on whether you are using the smaller version or the professional edition. These files are automatically loaded and integrated in your project (see the project window) when Visual Basic is started up. The automatic loading is performed by the start-up macro file called AUTOLOAD.MAK. This file is stored in the VB directory of Visual Basic. You can import additional controls into this file, or add them to the collection of tools according to your requirements. This is done by means of the *Add File* command from the *File* menu (Alt-F,D).

If the window containing the tools (or the corresponding icon) has disappeared behind other windows, you can open it by means of the *Toolbox* command from the *Window* menu (Alt-W,T). The toolbox control menu contains only two options:*Move* and *Close* (Alt-F4). Therefore it is not possible to enlarge or reduce this window.

Select a control by clicking on it. The 3D effect with shadows makes it appear as if that control button has been pressed.

All the examples you will encounter in this book have been created using the 22 controls of the Visual Basic Standard Edition.

POINTER
The activated Pointer enables you to drag an existing control to another position or to alter its size. You cannot create a control by using the Pointer; the appearance of the mouse pointer does not change into a cross as it does with the other controls.

PICTURE BOX

The Picture box control makes space within a form for the display of an illustration (bitmap, icon or metafile) which can be applied as an embellishment or as an active control. A Picture box can also be used to make a bitarray for grouping options which resemble one another in terms of either appearance or function. In addition, you can display the result of graphic commands in a Picture box, or text which has been created using the **Print** method.

LABEL

The Label control places a text which cannot be altered in a form. This can be for instance, a remark, a caption or an explanation. The text can only be modified during the execution of the program or during a DDE session.

TEXT BOX

The Text box control creates a field in which the program user can enter new text or can edit existing text.

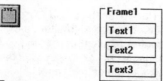

FRAME

The Frame control gathers controls together in a frame in order to improve the clarity of presentation. This is done on a basis of function resemblance. You can place short texts in the frame.

Note: Always make the frame first and then put the controls into it.

COMMAND BUTTON
The Command button control executes a command when the user activates this button. Examples of this type of control are the *OK* and *Cancel* buttons in dialog windows.

CHECK BOX
The Check box control is particularly suited to switching an option on or off. You can gather a number of these controls together into one group. In contrast to the option buttons (see below), several buttons may be activated at one time within the group.

OPTION BUTTON
The Option button control also switches an option on or off, but only one option button may be active within the group at one time, in contrast to the check box feature. When one option button is activated, the others are automatically switched off. This situation occurs for instance when you have to specify the paper size when working with a word processor.

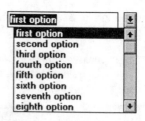

COMBO BOX

The Combo box control is a combination of an input box and an options list. Here, text can be entered or a choice can be made from a list of options shown. The list is either permanently visible or it can be opened by clicking on the arrow pointing downwards.

 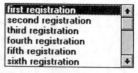

LIST BOX

The List box control generates a list of options from which a control can be selected. If there is not sufficient room for all the controls, a scroll bar appears automatically enabling you to browse through the list.

HORIZONTAL/VERTICAL SCROLL BAR

The Horizontal and Vertical scroll bar controls enable you to browse quickly through a long list or a large amount of information. When you are doing this, your current position is indicated by the position of the scroll block. A scroll bar is also extremely suited to making analogous parameters visible or to define these in terms of clarity, loudness etc.

TIMER

The Timer control implements a routine or a function after a specified interval. This control is not visible during the execution of a program, and can also be applied in processes taking place in the background. We used this control in the copyright windows in our Icon projects.

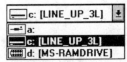

DRIVE LIST BOX

The Drive list box control indicates the active drive with which the application user is currently working. The arrow pointing downwards opens a list of drives which are available in the system. If the drives also have names, these are showed too, if the width of the list allows it.

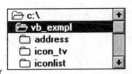

DIRECTORY LIST BOX

The Directory list box control generates an options list consisting of a hierarchical display of the directories in the currently active drive. This control enables the application user to switch to a different directory. If an extended directory tree does not fit into the list, a scroll bar appears automatically allowing the user to browse through the list.

FILE LIST BOX

The File list box control creates an options list in which the files with a specified extension (TXT for example)

are displayed. Just as with the extended directory tree,
a scroll bar appears automatically if the list is too long
to fit into the box.

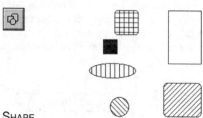

SHAPE
The Shape control adds a rectangle, a square, a
rounded square, an ellipse or a circle to a form. The
type of figure is chosen in the Properties window containing the *Shape* feature. Click on the control and then
on the Properties window. The filling is defined by
means of the *FillColor* and *FillStyle* options in the Properties window.

LINE
The Line control draws a horizontal, vertical or slanting
line in a form. The actual appearance of the line depends on the *DrawMode* property.

IMAGE
The Image control creates a space for displaying an
image (bitmap, icon or metafile). In contrast to a Picture box, the files in an Image control can only be displayed as an embellishment and not as an active element. However, the Image control does have the
advantage that it requires fewer system resources and
that the files are displayed more quickly.

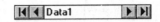

DATA

The Data control enables access to existing databanks in order to edit the information stored there in the application. In this way, files which have the Microsoft Access, dBASE, FoxPro, Paradox or Btrieve structure are accessible.

COMMON DIALOG

The Common dialog control generates one of the standard dialog windows, such as for opening, saving and printing files and for specifying colours or fonts for example.

 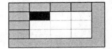

GRID

The Grid control creates a grid for a table with columns and rows. A text or an image can be placed in each cell, and both types of data can be edited by means of an application.

OLE 2.0

The OLE 2.0 control links an OLE object to the application or imports it (Object Linking and Embedding). This OLE technique enables you to display data from other Windows applications in your own programs. Clicking on the OLE control activates the application which created the object. For more information concerning OLE (available from version 3.1 onwards) and concerning the management of OLE objects, refer to the Windows manual.

The Properties window

Each form and each control has properties such as colour, size and position on the screen. The *Properties* window enables you to assign properties to an object. The properties and settings for the currently active form or control are displayed in this window. If you have activated several objects simultaneously (in combination with the Shift key), the list will show those properties which are shared: you can then alter these properties for all objects in one go if necessary.

Open the Properties window by clicking on the *Properties* option in the *Window* menu (Alt-W, O) or by pressing the F4 function key.

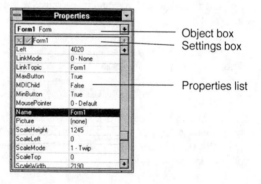

This window has three sections.

■ The *Object box* indicates the currently active form or control. If you wish to select a different control, use the scroll arrow to open the options list of the active form and all the controls in this form.

■ The *Settings box* enables you to alter the value of the activated property of the activated object. The scroll arrow at the right-hand side of the field opens a list of the values which are valid for this property. If the scroll arrow is (almost) invisible - as in our figure - you will have to type the required value of the property in the text box yourself. With some properties (such as BackColor), the scroll arrow is replaced by three dots. In that case, the button opens an additional options window. You accept the alteration (tick) or cancel it (cross) by clicking on the corresponding button to the left of the text field.

■ The *Properties list* (which may have a scroll arrow) of the form or object contains all the properties which can be altered. The left-hand column shows the names of the properties, the right-hand column shows their current values.

The Code window

Each project, and the forms and controls contained, consists of a large amount of commands, the so-called program code. Visual Basic has a program editor for adding and modifying functions and procedures. Various codes windows may be open simultaneously. There are four ways of activating a code window:

■ by double clicking on a control or on the form itself in the form window
■ by clicking on *Code* in the *View* menu (Alt-V,C) if an object has been marked
■ by pressing F7 if an object has been marked
■ by clicking on the *View Code* button in the Project window when a project object (the name of a form or module) has been selected.

The code window contains three fields:

■ By clicking on the scroll arrow at the right of the *Object box*, a list showing the current form and all the controls which are contained there. Select the name of an object from this list in order to adopt its program code into the large work area of the code window.
■ Select an event from the *Proc* box (*Procedure list box*) for the object you chose in the Object box. An *event* is a procedure which is caused or activated

Object box   Procedure list field

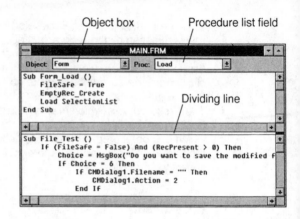

Dividing line

by the application user or the system, such as a keystroke or a click of the mouse button. This is called an *event procedure*. By clicking on *(general)* in the Object box, the general procedures which have been made for the current form, such as declarations, are displayed in the Procedures list box. A general procedure, in contrast to an event procedure, must be explicitly activated by an application. General procedures can be created both within the form code and within a module.
A general procedure within a form is only accessible from that form, but a general procedure within a module is accessible from every form.

■ The actual code window contains a *dividing line*. If you drag this line downwards, the window is divided into two independent work areas with their own scroll bars. The upper work area is closed if you drag the line upwards again.

Visual Basic designs the input automatically and, in addition, checks if the syntax is correct. On a colour monitor, the automatic design results in the keys words normally being shown in blue. The first letter of key words is always a capital letter. The syntax check produces a message if the program code is not valid, for example in cases where you type a comma where a semi-colon is necessary.

You can work quickly and effectively with a large number of keys or key combinations in the code window:

Key (combination)	Effect
F1	activate context-oriented help function
Ctrl-C	copy marked text to the Clipboard
Ctrl-X	remove marked text and place it in the Clipboard
Del	delete marked text
Ctrl-V	insert the contents of the Clipboard at the current cursor position
Cursor keys	move through the program code; mark when combined with Shift
Home	place cursor at the beginning of the line
End	place the cursor at the end of the line
Tab	indent the program code

The Project window

The Project window contains a summary of all forms, modules and extra controls which are part of the current project. This window is opened by clicking on the *Project* option in the *Window* menu (Alt-W, R).

The *View Form* button opens the marked form and the *View Code* button opens the code window containing the program code of the marked form or the marked module.

The Menu Design window

The *Menu Design* window enables you to design a menu for your application program. This is where you organize the order of sequence of the menus and the menu options and the hierarchy in these. In addition, you can allocate shortcuts and special features to the menu options. The Menu Design window is only available for an opened form.

Activate the form for which you want to create a menu and give the *Menu Design* command from the *Window* menu (Alt-W, M).

The Menu Design window is discussed in detail in section 5.2.

The colour palette

You can use the colour palette if you want to alter the colour of a form or a control, or if you wish to compile your own colour scheme. This window is opened by selecting *Color Palette* from the *Window* menu (Alt-W, C).

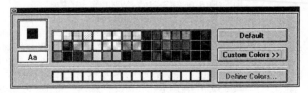

Environment and project options

The *Options* menu contains two options which open dialog windows. The *Environment* option opens a window which enables you to adapt the Visual Basic working environment to your own requirements. This includes such features as the tab stop settings, the syntax check switch, the default save format for files and the colours for the foreground and background in the code window. The *Reset* button restores the original setting of the current parameter, and *Reset All* restores the default settings of all parameters.

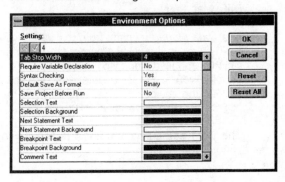

The *Options* menu also contains the *Project* option. Clicking on this produces the *Project Options* window. The parameters in this window only apply to the current project.

Behind the *Command Line Argument* parameter, type the parameters and switches for the start of the application, such as the name of a data file which is started along with the application. (These parameters and switches appear in the *Command Line* box of the *Program Item Properties* dialog window of the Program Manager. This window is activated by selecting *Properties* from the *File* menu or by pressing the shortcut key combination Alt-Enter.) You can also specify in this *Project Options* window which form should be loaded or displayed when the application is started, and also the name of your program's help file.

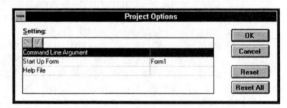

Data Manager

The *Data Manager* option from the *Window* menu (Alt-W,A) starts up the utility program for data management which is supplied along with Visual Basic. This program enables you to create a databank with the Microsoft Access format, or use existing files with the Access, dBASE, FoxPro, Paradox and Btrieve layout.

The Data Manager program is discussed in detail in chapter 7.

Appendix C
Program listings

The ICON_TV project

ICON_TV.FRM

```
Sub File1_Click ()
    File.Caption = File1.FileName
    Imidge.Picture = LoadPicture(File1.Path
⤷        & "\" & File1.FileName)
End Sub

Sub Form_Load ()
    Way.Caption = Dir1.Path
    File1.Pattern = "*.ico"
End Sub

Sub Drive1_Change ()
    Dir1.Path = Drive1.Drive
End Sub

Sub ProgEnd_Click ()
    End
End Sub

Sub Dir1_Change ()
    File1.Path = Dir1.Path
    Way.Caption = Dir1.Path
    File.Caption = ""
    Imidge.Picture = LoadPicture()
End Sub
```

The ICONLIST project

ICON_TV.FRM

```
Sub Imidge_DblClick ()
    If Right$(File1.FileName, 3) = "ico" Then
        Msg = "Bad Luck!" + Chr$(13) + "It is
            not possible to copy an icon file
            to the Clipboard."
        MsgBox Msg, 16
    Else
        ClipBoard.Clear
        ClipBoard.SetData Imidge.Picture
        M$ = "The file " +
            UCase$(File1.FileName) + " has been
            copied to the Clipboard."
        MsgBox M$, 48
    End If
End Sub


Sub File1_Click ()
    File.Caption = File1.FileName
    Imidge.Picture = LoadPicture(File1.Path &
        "\" & File1.FileName)
End Sub


Sub Extension_Click ()
    Select Case (Extension.ListIndex)
        Case 0
            File1.Pattern = "*.ico"
        Case 1
            File1.Pattern = "*.bmp"
        Case 2
            File1.Pattern = "*.wmf"
        Case 3
            File1.Pattern = "*.ico; *.bmp;
                *.wmf"
    End Select
    Dir1_Change
End Sub
```

```
Sub Form_Load ()
    Extension.AddItem "Icon (*.ICO)"
    Extension.AddItem "Bitmap (*.BMP)"
    Extension.AddItem "Metafile (*.WMF)"
    Extension.AddItem "All files"
    Extension.ListIndex = 0
    Way.Caption = Dir1.Path
    File1.Pattern = "*.ico"
    Dir1_Change
End Sub


Sub IconSwitch_Click ()
    If (File1.ListCount) > 0 Then
        MousePointer = 11
        IconList.Show 1
    Else
        FM$ = "No " + UCase$(File1.Pattern) +
↻           " files found."
        MsgBox FM$, 48
    End If
    MousePointer = 0
End Sub


Sub Info_Click ()
    InfoWindow.Show 1
End Sub


Sub Drive1_Change ()
    On Error GoTo Drive1_Change_ErrorMessage
    Dir1.Path = Drive1.Drive
Exit Sub
Drive1_Change_ErrorMessage:
    Select Case Err
        Case 68
            Msg = " Drive " +
↻               UCase$(Drive1.Drive) +
↻               " unavailable. "
```

```
        Case 70 To 71
            Msg = Error$
        Case Else
            Msg = Str$(Err) + " : " + Error$
    End Select
    MsgBox Msg, 16
    Drive1.Drive = Dir1.Path
    Resume Next
End Sub


Sub ProgEnd_Click ()
    End
End Sub


Sub Dir1_Change ()
    File1.Path = Dir1.Path
    Route1$ = File1.Path
    FNameNr = File1.ListCount
    Way.Caption = Dir1.Path
    If File1.ListCount > 0 Then
        For Index = 0 To File1.ListCount - 1
            Fylename(Index) = File1.List(Index)
        Next Index
    End If
    File.Caption = ""
    Imidge.Picture = LoadPicture()
End Sub


Sub Dir1_KeyPress (KeyAnsi As Integer)
    If KeyAnsi = 13 Then
    Dir1.Path = Dir1.List(Dir1.ListIndex)
    File1.Path = Dir1.Path
    End If
End Sub
```

ICONLIST.FRM

```
Dim BWaarde As Integer

Sub Windows_Fill ()
MousePointer = 11
    Grid = 1500
    PosFromLeft = 50
    PosFromTop = 750

    IconsPerRow = Int((IconList.ScaleWidth - 50
⊋       - VertScroll.Width) / Grid)
    IconRows = Int((IconList.ScaleHeight - 750)
⊋       / Raster)
    WindowFull = IconsPerRow * IconRows

    If FNameNr <= WindowFull Then
        BValue = 1
        VertScroll.Enabled = False
    Else
        VertScroll.Enabled = True
    End If

    EValue = BValue + (WindowFull - 1)

    If EValue > FNameNr Then
        EValue = FNameNr
    End If

    If (FNameNr - BValue) < WindowFull Then
        VertScroll.Max = BValue
    Else
        VertScroll.Max = FNameNr
    End If

    VertScroll.SmallChange = IconsPerRow
    VertScroll.LargeChange = WindowFull

    For Index = BValue To EValue
        FirstOut.Caption = BValue
        LastOut.Caption = EValue
```

```
            FNumOut.Caption = FNameNr
            ImageList(Index).Left = PosFromLeft +
↻              300
            ImageList(Index).Top = PosFromTop
            ImageList(Index).Visible = True
            IconFileList(Index).Left = PosFromLeft
            IconFileList(Index).Top = PosFromTop +
↻              1050
            IconFileList(Index).Visible = True

            If (PosFromLeft + Grid +
↻              IconFileList(Index).Width >
↻              IconList.ScaleWidth) Then
                PosFromLeft = 50
                PosFromTop = PosFromTop + Grid
            Else
                PosFromLeft = PosFromLeft + Grid
            End If
    Next Index
    MousePointer = 0
End Sub


Sub Icons_Invisible ()
    For Index = 1 To FNameNr
        ImageList(Index).Visible = False
        IconFileList(Index).Visible = False
    Next Index
End Sub


Sub ImageList_DblClick (Index As Integer)
    If Right$(Fylename(Index - 1), 3) =
↻        "ico" Then
        Msg = "Bad Luck!" + Chr$(13) + "It is
↻          not possible to copy an icon file
↻          to the Clipboard."
        MsgBox Msg, 16
    Else
        ClipBoard.Clear
```

```
          ClipBoard.SetData
              ImageList(Index).Picture
          M$ = "The file    " +
              UCase$(Fylename(Index - 1)) +
              "   has been copied to the
              Clipboard."
          MsgBox M$, 48
      End If
  End Sub


  Sub Form_Load ()
      MousePointer = 11
          For Index = FNameNr To 1 Step -1
              Load ImageList(Index)
              ImageList(Index).Picture =
                  LoadPicture(Route1$ + "\" +
                  Fylename(Index - 1))
              Load IconFileList(Index)
              IconFileList(Index).Caption =
                  Fylename(Index - 1)
          Next Index
      MousePointer = 0
      BValue = 1
      Windows_Fill
  End Sub


  Sub Form_Resize ()
      If IconList.Height <= 2750 Then
          IconList.Height = 2750
      If IconList.Width <= 2750 Then
          IconList.Width = 2750
      VertScroll.Top = IconList.ScaleTop +
          TopLine.Height
      VertScroll.Left = IconList.ScaleWidth -
          VertScroll.Width
      VertScroll.Height = IconList.ScaleHeight-
          TopLine.Height
      Icons_Invisible
      Windows_Fill
  End Sub
```

```
Sub IconListClose_Click ()
    Unload IconList
End Sub


Sub VertScroll_Change ()
    Icons_Invisible
    BValue = VertScroll.Value
    Windows_Fill
End Sub
```

INFO.FRM

```
Sub InfoBOK_Click ()
    Unload InfoWindow
End Sub


Sub Timer1_Timer ()
    Static MouthOpen As Integer
    If MouthOpen Then
        InfoIcon.Picture = IMouthOpen.Picture
    Else
        InfoIcon.Picture = IMouthShut.Picture
    End If
    MouthOpen = Not MouthOpen
End Sub
```

GLOBAL1.BAS

```
Global Route1$
Global Fylename(0 To 255)
Global FNameNr As Integer
```

The MC project (Music Catalogue)

SELECT.FRM

```
Sub SelectBOK_Click ()
    Fill_Overview
    SelectionList.Hide
End Sub
```

MAIN.FRM

```
Sub File_Test ()
    If (FileSafe = False) And (RecPresent > 0)
        Then
        Choice = MsgBox("Do you want to save
            the modified file?", 36)
        If Choice = 6 Then
            If CMDialog1.Filename = "" Then
                CMDialog1.Action = 2
            End If
            Memory_To_Disk
        End If
    End If
    FileSafe = True
End Sub


Sub Print_Records ()
MousePointer = 11
Dim PageNumber As Integer
    For NumCopies = 1 To CMDialog1.Copies
        Printer.FontName = Overview.FontName
        Printer.FontSize = 12
        PageNumber = 1
        For RecNr = 1 To RecPresent
            If RecNr Mod 52 = 1 Then
                Printer.Print
                Printer.Print
```

```
                    Printer.Print Tab(6);
                        "Music Catalogue V1.00";
                    Printer.Print Tab(33);
                        CMDialog1.Filetitle;
                    Printer.Print Tab(54);
                        RecPresent;
                    Printer.Print Tab(59);
                        "records";
                    Printer.Print Tab(73);
                        Format$(Now, "dd.mm.yy");
                    Printer.Print Tab(86); "Page";
                    Printer.Print Tab(92);
                        PageNumber
                    Printer.Print
                    Printer.Print Tab(6); "ARTIST";
                    Printer.Print Tab(40); "TITLE";
                    Printer.Print Tab(73); "TYPE";
                    Printer.Print Tab(81); "#";
                    Printer.Print Tab(86); "GENRE"
                    Printer.Print
                End If
                Printer.Print Tab(6);
                    Left$(MusicRec(RecNr).Artist,25);
                Printer.Print Tab(40);
                    Left$(MusicRec(RecNr).Title,25);
                Select Case MusicRec(RecNr).Type
                    Case 0
                        Printer.Print Tab(73); "CD";
                    Case 1
                        Printer.Print Tab(73); "LP";
                    Case 2
                        Printer.Print Tab(73); "MC";
                    Case 3
                        Printer.Print Tab(73); "DAT";
                End Select
                Printer.Print Tab(81);
                    Left$(MusicRec(RecNr).Quantity, 2)
                Printer.Print Tab(86);
                    Left$(MusicRec(RecNr).Genre, 12);
                If RecNr Mod 52 = 0 Then
                    Printer.NewPage
```

```
                PageNumber = PageNumber + 1
            End If
        Next RecNr
        If RecPresent Mod 52 <> 0 Then
            Printer.NewPage
        End If
        Printer.EndDoc
    Next NumCopies
MousePointer = 0
End Sub


Sub EditMenu_Click ()
    Mask.Show 1
End Sub


Sub Form_Load ()
    FileSafe = True
    EmptyRec_Create
    Load SelectionList
End Sub


Sub Form_Resize ()
    If (MusicMain.Height > 2000) And
↻       (MusicMain.Width > 2000) Then
        Overview.Height = MusicMain.ScaleHeight
↻           - StatusLine.Height
        Overview.Width = MusicMain.ScaleWidth
    End If
End Sub


Sub Overview_Click ()
    CurRec = Overview.SelStartRow
    StatusLine_Modify
End Sub
```

```
Sub Overview_DblClick ()
    CurRec = Overview.SelStartRow
    StatusLine_Modify
    Mask.Show 1
End Sub


Sub Overview_KeyDown ()
    CurRec = Overview.SelStartRow
    StatusLine_Modify
End Sub


Sub Overview_KeyUp ()
    CurRec = Overview.SelStartRow
    StatusLine_Modify
End Sub


Sub Overview_MouseDown (Button As Integer,
⇨    Shift As Integer, X As Single, Y As Single)
    If Button = 2 Then
        PopupMenu EditMenu
    End If
End Sub


Sub MView_Click (Index As Integer)
On Error GoTo ErrCanc
Select Case Index
    Case 0
        If MView(0).Checked = False Then
            MView(0).Checked = True
            StatusLine.Visible = True
        Else
            MView(0).Checked = False
            StatusLine.Visible = False
        End If
    Case 1
        If MView(1).Checked = False Then
            MView(1).Checked = True
```

```
                    Fill_Overview
                    Overview.Visible = True
            Else
                    MView(1).Checked = False
                    Overview.Visible = False
            End If
            Menu_Operate
        Case 3
            SelectionList.Show 1
        Case 4
            CMDialog1.Flags = &H28103
            CMDialog1.Action = 4
            Overview.FontName = CMDialog1.FontName
            Overview.FontSize = CMDialog1.FontSize
            Overview.FontBold = CMDialog1.FontBold
            Overview.FontItalic =
            CMDialog1.FontItalic
            Overview.FontUnderline =
            CMDialog1.FontUnderline
            Overview.FontStrikethru =
            CMDialog1.FontStrikethru
            Overview.ForeColor = CMDialog1.Color
        Case 6
            CMDialog1.Action = 3
            Overview.BackColor = CMDialog1.Color
    End Select
ErrCanc:
    Exit Sub
End Sub


Sub MFile_Click (Index As Integer)
On Error GoTo MisCanc
    Select Case Index
        Case 0
            File_Test
            RecPresent = 0
            Menu_Operate
            CMDialog1.Filename = ""
            RecPresent = 1
            CurRec = 1
```

```
                MusicRec(1) = EmptyRec
                StatusLine_Modify
                Mask.Show 1
            Case 1
                File_Test
                CMDialog1.Action = 1
                Disk_To_Memory
                Menu_Operate
                Fill_Overview
            Case 2
                If CMDialog1.Filename = "" Then
                    CMDialog1.Action = 1
                End If
                Memory_To_Disk
            Case 3
                CMDialog1.Action = 2
                Memory_To_Disk
            Case 5
                CMDialog1.Flags = &H10000C
                CMDialog1.Action = 5
                Print_Records
            Case 7
                File_Test
                End
        End Select
    MisCanc:
        Exit Sub
    End Sub


    Sub MInfo_Click (Index As Integer)
        InfoWindow.Show 1
    End Sub


    Sub MLetter_Click (Index As Integer)
        Select Case Index
            Case 0
                Overview.FontSize = 8
            Case 1
                Overview.FontSize = 10
```

```
        Case 2
            Overview.FontSize = 12
        Case 3
            Overview.FontSize = 14
    End Select
End Sub
```

INFO.FRM

```
Sub InfoBOK_Click ()
    Unload InfoWindow
End Sub
```

MASK.FRM

```
Sub Rec_Incomp ()
    MsgBox "Incomplete record." + Chr$(13) +
↻       "Enter the name of the artist.", 48
    MaskArtist.SetFocus
End Sub


Sub Form_Load ()
    FileSafe = False
    MaskRec = MusicRec(CurRec)
    MaskRec_To_Fields
    MaskGenre.AddItem "Rock"
    MaskGenre.AddItem "Pop"
    MaskGenre.AddItem "Blues"
    MaskGenre.AddItem "Jazz"
    MaskGenre.AddItem "Heavy Metal"
    MaskGenre.AddItem "Funk"
    MaskGenre.AddItem "Classical"
    MaskGenre.AddItem "Soul"
    MaskGenre.AddItem "Folk"
    MaskGenre.AddItem "Country"
    MaskGenre.AddItem "Rap"
    MaskGenre.AddItem "World Music"
    MaskGenre.AddItem "Hard Rock"
```

```
        MaskGenre.AddItem "Punk"
        MaskGenre.AddItem "Soundtrack"
        MaskGenre.AddItem "Swing"
        MaskGenre.AddItem "Synthesizer"
        MaskGenre.AddItem "Reggae"
        MaskGenre.AddItem "House"
        MaskGenre.AddItem "Techno"
        MaskGenre.AddItem "Disco"
        MaskGenre.AddItem "Soft Rock"
        MaskGenre.AddItem "Rock 'n' Roll"
        MaskGenre.AddItem "Thrash Metal"
        MaskGenre.AddItem "Experimental"
        MaskGenre.AddItem "Unknown"
    End Sub



    Sub MaskQuantity_GotFocus ()
        MaskQuantity.SelStart = 0
        MaskQuantity.SelLength =
 ↳         Len(MaskQuantity.Text)
    End Sub



    Sub MaskBCancel_Click ()
        MousePointer = 11
        If (Trim$(MaskArtist.Text) = "") And
 ↳         (CurRec = RecPresent) Then
            RecPresent = RecPresent - 1
            CurRec = RecPresent
        End If
        Sort_Artist
        StatusLine_Modify
        Menu_Operate
        Fill_Overview
        Unload Mask
        MousePointer = 0
    End Sub



    Sub MaskBREnd_Click ()
        If Trim$(MaskArtist.Text) <> "" Then
```

```
            Fields_To_MaskRec
            MusicRec(CurRec) = MaskRec
            CurRec = RecPresent
            MaskRec = MusicRec(CurRec)
            MaskRec_To_Fields
        Else
            Rec_Incomp
        End If
        StatusLine_Modify
    End Sub


    Sub MaskBRBegin_Click ()
        If Trim$(MaskArtist.Text) <> "" Then
            Fields_To_MaskRec
            MusicRec(CurRec) = MaskRec
            CurRec = 1
            MaskRec = MusicRec(CurRec)
            MaskRec_To_Fields
        Else
            Rec_Incomp
        End If
        StatusLine_Modify
    End Sub


    Sub MaskBClose_Click ()
        MousePointer = 11
        If Trim$(MaskArtist.Text) <> "" Then
            Fields_To_MaskRec
            MusicRec(CurRec) = MaskRec
            Sort_Artist
            Unload Mask
        Else
            Rec_Incomp
        End If
        StatusLine_Modify
        Menu_Operate
        Fill_Overview
        MousePointer = 0
    End Sub
```

```
Sub MaskBRNext_Click ()
    If CurRec < RecPresent Then
        If Trim$(MaskArtist.Text) <> "" Then
            Fields_To_MaskRec
            MusicRec(CurRec) = MaskRec
            CurRec = CurRec + 1
            MaskRec = MusicRec(CurRec)
            MaskRec_To_Fields
        Else
            Rec_Incomp
        End If
    Else
        MsgBox "End of file.", 64
    End If
    StatusLine_Modify
End Sub


Sub MaskBRPrevious_Click ()
    If CurRec > 1 Then
        If Trim$(MaskArtist.Text) <> "" Then
            Fields_To_MaskRec
            MusicRec(CurRec) = MaskRec
            CurRec = CurRec - 1
            MaskRec = MusicRec(CurRec)
            MaskRec_To_Fields
        Else
            Rec_Incomp
        End If
    Else
        MsgBox "Beginning of the file.", 64
    End If
    StatusLine_Modify
End Sub


Sub MaskNotes_GotFocus ()
    MaskNotes.SelStart = 0
    MaskNotes.SelLength = Len(MaskNotes.Text)
End Sub
```

```
Sub MaskBCopy_Click ()
    If RecPresent < MaxRecNum Then
        If Trim$(MaskArtist.Text) <> "" Then
            Fields_To_MaskRec
            MusicRec(CurRec) = MaskRec
            RecPresent = RecPresent + 1
            CurRec = RecPresent
        Else
            Rec_Incomp
        End If
    Else
        MsgBox "There are no more available
            records.", 48
    End If
    StatusLine_Modify
    MaskArtist.SetFocus
End Sub


Sub MaskBDelete_Click ()
    Choice = MsgBox("Do you really want to
        delete the record?", 36)
    If Choice = 6 Then
        If RecPresent = 1 Then
            MaskRec = EmptyRec
            MusicRec(CurRec) = MaskRec
            MaskRec_To_Fields
        Else
            If CurRec = RecPresent Then
                MaskRec = EmptyRec
                MusicRec(CurRec) = MaskRec
                RecPresent = RecPresent - 1
                CurRec = RecPresent
                MaskRec = MusicRec(CurRec)
                MaskRec_To_Fields
            Else
                For RecNr = CurRec
                    To RecPresent - 1
                MusicRec(RecNr) =
                    MusicRec(RecNr + 1)
                Next RecNr
```

```
                    MaskRec = EmptyRec
                    MusicRec(RecPresent) = MaskRec
                    RecPresent = RecPresent - 1
                    MaskRec = MusicRec(CurRec)
                    MaskRec_To_Fields
                End If
            End If
        End If
        StatusLine_Modify
        MaskArtist.SetFocus
    End Sub


    Sub MaskBNew_Click ()
        If RecPresent < MaxRecNum Then
            If Trim$(MaskArtist.Text) <> "" Then
                Fields_To_MaskRec
                MusicRec(CurRec) = MaskRec
                RecPresent = RecPresent + 1
                CurRec = RecPresent
                MaskRec = EmptyRec
                MaskRec_To_Fields
            Else
                Rec_Incomp
            End If
        Else
            MsgBox "There are no more available
                records.", 48
        End If
        StatusLine_Modify
        MaskArtist.SetFocus
    End Sub


    Sub MaskArtist_GotFocus ()
        MaskArtist.SelStart = 0
        MaskArtist.SelLength = Len(MaskArtist.Text)
    End Sub
```

```
Sub MaskGenre_GotFocus ()
    MaskGenre.SelStart = 0
    MaskGenre.SelLength = Len(MaskGenre.Text)
End Sub


Sub MaskTitle_GotFocus ()
    MaskTitle.SelStart = 0
    MaskTitle.SelLength = Len(MaskTitle.Text)
End Sub
```

GLOBAL.BAS

```
Type Record
    Artist As String * 30
    Title As String * 30
    Type As Integer
    Quantity As String * 2
    Genre As String * 15
    Notes As String * 200
End Type
Global Const MaxRecNum = 500
Global MusicRec(MaxRecNum) As Record
Global RecPresent As Integer
Global CurRec As Integer
Global EmptyRec As Record
Global MaskRec As Record
Global SwapRec As Record
Global FileSafe As Integer


Sub Fields_To_MaskRec ()
    MaskRec.Artist =
↻        LTrim$(Mask.MaskArtist.Text)
    MaskRec.Title =
↻        LTrim$(Mask.MaskTitle.Text)
    For TypeIndex = 0 To 3
        If Mask.MaskOption(TypeIndex).Value
↻            = True Then
            MaskRec.Type = TypeIndex
```

```
            End If
        Next TypeIndex
        MaskRec.Quantity =
↺           LTrim$(Mask.MaskQuantity.Text)
        MaskRec.Genre =
↺           LTrim$(Mask.MaskGenre.Text)
        MaskRec.Notes =
↺           LTrim$(Mask.MaskNotes.Text)
    End Sub


    Sub Sort_Artist ()
    Dim SortFlag As Integer
        If RecPresent > 1 Then
            Do
                MousePointer = 11
                SortFlag = False
                For RecNr = 1 To RecPresent - 1
                    If Trim$(MusicRec(RecNr).Artist) >
↺                       (MusicRec(RecNr + 1).Artist)
↺                       Then
                        SwapRec = MusicRec(RecNr)
                        MusicRec(RecNr) =
↺                           MusicRec(RecNr + 1)
                        MusicRec(RecNr + 1) = SwapRec
                        SortFlag = True
                    End If
                Next RecNr
            Loop Until SortFlag = False
        End If
        If CurRec = RecPresent Then
            CurRec = 1
        End If
        MousePointer = 0
    End Sub


    Sub EmptyRec_Create ()
        EmptyRec.Artist = ""
        EmptyRec.Title = ""
        EmptyRec.Type = 0
```

```
        EmptyRec.Quantity = "1"
        EmptyRec.Genre = ""
        EmptyRec.Notes = ""
End Sub


Sub Fill_Overview ()
MousePointer = 11
        MusicMain.Overview.Cols = 7
        MusicMain.Overview.Rows = RecPresent + 1
        MusicMain.Overview.FixedAlignment(0) = 2
        MusicMain.Overview.ColWidth(0) = 400
        MusicMain.Overview.Row = 0
        MusicMain.Overview.Col = 1
        If SelectionList.Selection(0) = 1 Then
            MusicMain.Overview.ColWidth(1) = 2000
        Else
            MusicMain.Overview.ColWidth(1) = 1
        End If
        MusicMain.Overview.Text = "Artist"
        MusicMain.Overview.Col = 2
        If SelectionList.Selection(1) = 1 Then
            MusicMain.Overview.ColWidth(2) = 2000
        Else
            MusicMain.Overview.ColWidth(2) = 1
        End If
        MusicMain.Overview.Text = "Title"
        MusicMain.Overview.Col = 3
        If SelectionList.Selection(2) = 1 Then
            MusicMain.Overview.ColWidth(3) = 400
        Else
            MusicMain.Overview.ColWidth(3) = 1
        End If
        MusicMain.Overview.Text = "Type"
        MusicMain.Overview.Col = 4
        MusicMain.Overview.ColAlignment(4) = 2
        If SelectionList.Selection(3) = 1 Then
            MusicMain.Overview.ColWidth(4) = 400
        Else
            MusicMain.Overview.ColWidth(4) = 1
        End If
```

```
        MusicMain.Overview.Text = "Set"
        MusicMain.Overview.Col = 5
        If SelectionList.Selection(4) = 1 Then
            MusicMain.Overview.ColWidth(5) = 2000
        Else
            MusicMain.Overview.ColWidth(5) = 1
        End If
        MusicMain.Overview.Text = "Genre"
        MusicMain.Overview.Col = 6
        MusicMain.Overview.ColWidth(6) = 5000
        MusicMain.Overview.Text = "Notes"
        For RecNr = 1 To RecPresent
            MusicMain.Overview.Col = 0
            MusicMain.Overview.Row = RecNr
            MusicMain.Overview.Text = RecNr
            MusicMain.Overview.SelStartCol = 1
            MusicMain.Overview.SelStartRow = RecNr
            MusicMain.Overview.SelEndCol = 6
            MusicMain.Overview.SelEndRow = RecNr
            MusicMain.Overview.Clip =
↺               MusicRec(RecNr).Artist +Chr$(.9)
↺               +MusicRec(RecNr).Title +Chr$(9)
↺               +"" +Chr$(9) +MusicRec(RecNr).Genre
↺               +Chr$(9) +MusicRec(RecNr).Notes
            MusicMain.Overview.Col = 3
            Select Case MusicRec(RecNr).Type
                Case 0
                    MusicMain.Overview.Text = "CD"
                Case 1
                    MusicMain.Overview.Text = "LP"
                Case 2
                    MusicMain.Overview.Text = "MC"
                Case 3
                    MusicMain.Overview.Text = "DAT"
            End Select
        Next RecNr
    MusicMain.Overview.SelStartCol = 1
    MusicMain.Overview.SelStartRow = CurRec
    MusicMain.Overview.SelEndCol = 6
    MusicMain.Overview.SelEndRow = CurRec
MousePointer = 0
End Sub
```

```
Sub MaskRec_To_Fields ()
    Mask.MaskArtist.Text =
        RTrim$(MaskRec.Artist)
    Mask.MaskTitle.Text = RTrim$(MaskRec.Title)
    Mask.MaskOption(MaskRec.Type).Value = True
    Mask.MaskQuantity.Text =
        RTrim$(MaskRec.Quantity)
    Mask.MaskGenre.Text = RTrim$(MaskRec.Genre)
    Mask.MaskNotes.Text =
        RTrim$(MaskRec.Notes)
End Sub



Sub Menu_Operate ()
    If RecPresent > 0 Then
        MusicMain.MFile(2).Enabled = True
        MusicMain.MFile(3).Enabled = True
        MusicMain.MFile(5).Enabled = True
        MusicMain.EditMenu.Enabled = True
        MusicMain.MView(1).Enabled = True
    Else
        MusicMain.MFile(2).Enabled = False
        MusicMain.MFile(3).Enabled = False
        MusicMain.MFile(5).Enabled = False
        MusicMain.EditMenu.Enabled = False
        MusicMain.MView(1).Enabled = False
        MusicMain.MView(1).Checked = False
        MusicMain.Overview.Visible = False
    End If
    If MusicMain.MView(1).Checked = True Then
        MusicMain.MView(3).Enabled = True
        MusicMain.MView(4).Enabled = True
        MusicMain.MView(5).Enabled = True
        MusicMain.MView(6).Enabled = True
    Else
        MusicMain.MView(3).Enabled = False
        MusicMain.MView(4).Enabled = False
        MusicMain.MView(5).Enabled = False
        MusicMain.MView(6).Enabled = False
    End If
End Sub
```

```
Sub Disk_To_Memory ()
    MousePointer = 11
    Open MusicMain.CMDialog1.Filename
↻        For Input As #1
    If Input$(6, #1) <> "MC1.00" Then
        MsgBox "File cannot be loaded."
↻        + Chr$(13) + "INCORRECT FILE FORMAT", 48
        Close #1
        Exit Sub
    End If
    Input #1, RecPresent
    For RecNr = 1 To RecPresent
        MusicRec(RecNr).Artist = Input$(30, #1)
        MusicRec(RecNr).Title = Input$(30, #1)
        Input #1, MusicRec(RecNr).Type
        MusicRec(RecNr).Quantity = Input$(2, #1)
        MusicRec(RecNr).Genre = Input$(15, #1)
        MusicRec(RecNr).Notes = Input$(200, #1)
    Next RecNr
    Close #1
    CurRec = 1
    StatusLine_Modify
    MousePointer = 0
End Sub


Sub Memory_To_Disk ()
    MousePointer = 11
    Open MusicMain.CMDialog1.Filename
↻        For Output As #1
    Print #1, "MC1.00";
    Print #1, RecPresent;
    For RecNr = 1 To RecPresent
        Print #1, MusicRec(RecNr).Artist;
        Print #1, MusicRec(RecNr).Title;
        Print #1, MusicRec(RecNr).Type;
        Print #1, MusicRec(RecNr).Quantity;
        Print #1, MusicRec(RecNr).Genre;
        Print #1, MusicRec(RecNr).Notes;
    Next RecNr
    Close #1
```

```
        StatusLine_Modify
        MousePointer = 0
    FileSafe = True
    End Sub


    Sub StatusLine_Modify ()
        MusicMain.StatusFile.Caption = "File: " +
↺       UCase$(MusicMain.CMDialog1.Filename)
        MusicMain.StatusRecord.Caption = "Record: " +
↺       Str$(CurRec) + " of " + Str$(RecPresent)
    End Sub
```

The ADDRESS project

ADDRESS.FRM

```
Sub ABClose_Click ()
    End
End Sub


Sub ABAdd_Click ()
    Data1.Caption = "Add new record"
    Data1.Recordset.AddNew
    AName.SetFocus
End Sub


Sub ABDelete_Click ()
    Answer = MsgBox("Do you really want to
↺       delete the record?", 20)
    If Answer = 6 Then
        Data1.Recordset.Delete
        Data1.Recordset.MovePrevious
        If Data1.Recordset.BOF = True Then
            Data1.Recordset.MoveNext
        End If
    End If
    AName.SetFocus
End Sub
```

```
Sub ABSearch_Click ()
    SearchFm.Show 1
    AName.SetFocus
End Sub


Sub Datal_MouseDown (Button As Integer, Shift As
↪    Integer, X As Single, Y As Single)
    Datal.Caption = "Modify record"
End Sub


Sub Form_Load ()
    Datal.Caption = "Modify record"
End Sub
```

SEARCH.FRM

```
Sub SearchBCanc_Click ()
    Unload SearchFm
End Sub


Sub SearchBOK_Click ()
    AddressForm.Datal.RecordSet.FindFirst "Name
↪        Like '" + SearchText.Text + "*' or
↪        Forename Like '" + SearchText.Text +
↪        "*'"
    Unload SearchFm
End Sub
```

Appendix D
ANSI table

Dec	Hex	Chr	Dec	Hex	Chr	Dec	Hex	Chr	Dec	Hex	Chr	Dec	Hex	Chr	Dec	Hex	Chr	Dec	Hex	Chr	Dec	Hex	Chr
0	0	.	32	20		64	40	@	96	60	`	128	80	.	160	A0		192	C0	À	224	E0	à
1	1	.	33	21	!	65	41	A	97	61	a	129	81	.	161	A1	¡	193	C1	Á	225	E1	á
2	2	.	34	22	"	66	42	B	98	62	b	130	82	.	162	A2	¢	194	C2	Â	226	E2	â
3	3	.	35	23	#	67	43	C	99	63	c	131	83	.	163	A3	£	195	C3	Ã	227	E3	ã
4	4	.	36	24	$	68	44	D	100	64	d	132	84	.	164	A4	¤	196	C4	Ä	228	E4	ä
5	5	.	37	25	%	69	45	E	101	65	e	133	85	.	165	A5	¥	197	C5	Å	229	E5	å
6	6	.	38	26	&	70	46	F	102	66	f	134	86	.	166	A6	¦	198	C6	Æ	230	E6	æ
7	7	.	39	27	'	71	47	G	103	67	g	135	87	.	167	A7	§	199	C7	Ç	231	E7	ç
8	8	.	40	28	(	72	48	H	104	68	h	136	88	.	168	A8	¨	200	C8	È	232	E8	è
9	9	.	41	29	)	73	49	I	105	69	i	137	89	.	169	A9	©	201	C9	É	233	E9	é
10	A	.	42	2A	*	74	4A	J	106	6A	j	138	8A	.	170	AA	ª	202	CA	Ê	234	EA	ê
11	B	.	43	2B	+	75	4B	K	107	6B	k	139	8B	.	171	AB	«	203	CB	Ë	235	EB	ë
12	C	.	44	2C	,	76	4C	L	108	6C	l	140	8C	.	172	AC	¬	204	CC	Ì	236	EC	ì
13	D	.	45	2D	-	77	4D	M	109	6D	m	141	8D	.	173	AD		205	CD	Í	237	ED	í
14	E	.	46	2E	.	78	4E	N	110	6E	n	142	8E	.	174	AE	®	206	CE	Î	238	EE	î
15	F	.	47	2F	/	79	4F	O	111	6F	o	143	8F	.	175	AF	¯	207	CF	Ï	239	EF	ï
16	10	.	48	30	0	80	50	P	112	70	p	144	90	.	176	B0	°	208	D0	Ð	240	F0	ð
17	11	.	49	31	1	81	51	Q	113	71	q	145	91	'	177	B1	±	209	D1	Ñ	241	F1	ñ
18	12	.	50	32	2	82	52	R	114	72	r	146	92	'	178	B2	²	210	D2	Ò	242	F2	ò
19	13	.	51	33	3	83	53	S	115	73	s	147	93	"	179	B3	³	211	D3	Ó	243	F3	ó
20	14	.	52	34	4	84	54	T	116	74	t	148	94	"	180	B4	´	212	D4	Ô	244	F4	ô
21	15	.	53	35	5	85	55	U	117	75	u	149	95	•	181	B5	µ	213	D5	Õ	245	F5	õ
22	16	.	54	36	6	86	56	V	118	76	v	150	96	–	182	B6	¶	214	D6	Ö	246	F6	ö
23	17	.	55	37	7	87	57	W	119	77	w	151	97	—	183	B7	·	215	D7	×	247	F7	÷
24	18	.	56	38	8	88	58	X	120	78	x	152	98	.	184	B8	¸	216	D8	Ø	248	F8	ø
25	19	.	57	39	9	89	59	Y	121	79	y	153	99	.	185	B9	¹	217	D9	Ù	249	F9	ù
26	1A	.	58	3A	:	90	5A	Z	122	7A	z	154	9A	.	186	BA	º	218	DA	Ú	250	FA	ú
27	1B	.	59	3B	;	91	5B	[	123	7B	{	155	9B	.	187	BB	»	219	DB	Û	251	FB	û
28	1C	.	60	3C	<	92	5C	\	124	7C	|	156	9C	.	188	BC	¼	220	DC	Ü	252	FC	ü
29	1D	.	61	3D	=	93	5D	]	125	7D	}	157	9D	.	189	BD	½	221	DD	Ý	253	FD	ý
30	1E	.	62	3E	>	94	5E	^	126	7E	~	158	9E	.	190	BE	¾	222	DE	Þ	254	FE	þ
31	1F	.	63	3F	?	95	5F	_	127	7F		159	9F	.	191	BF	¿	223	DF	ß	255	FF	ÿ

Index